NAUPAKA

A book about loss, leaving, and returning

Lideweij Bosman

NAUPAKA

Liinkt

Published by LIINKT
First edition, 2014

Illustrations by Floor Rieder
Book design by Roel Geurts, Breda
Author photograph by Masha Osipova

Editors: Manon van Wijnen, Esmir van Wering

© 2020 Bosman, Lideweij
Herstellung und Verlag: BoD – Books on Demand, Norderstedt
ISBN: 9783752820430

Translation copyright © 2014 by Annoesjka Oostindiër

FOR YOU, SANDER.

NI'IHAU
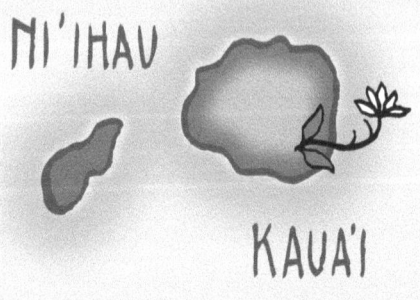
KAUA'I

O'AHU

HONOLULU

pacific ocean

HAWAII

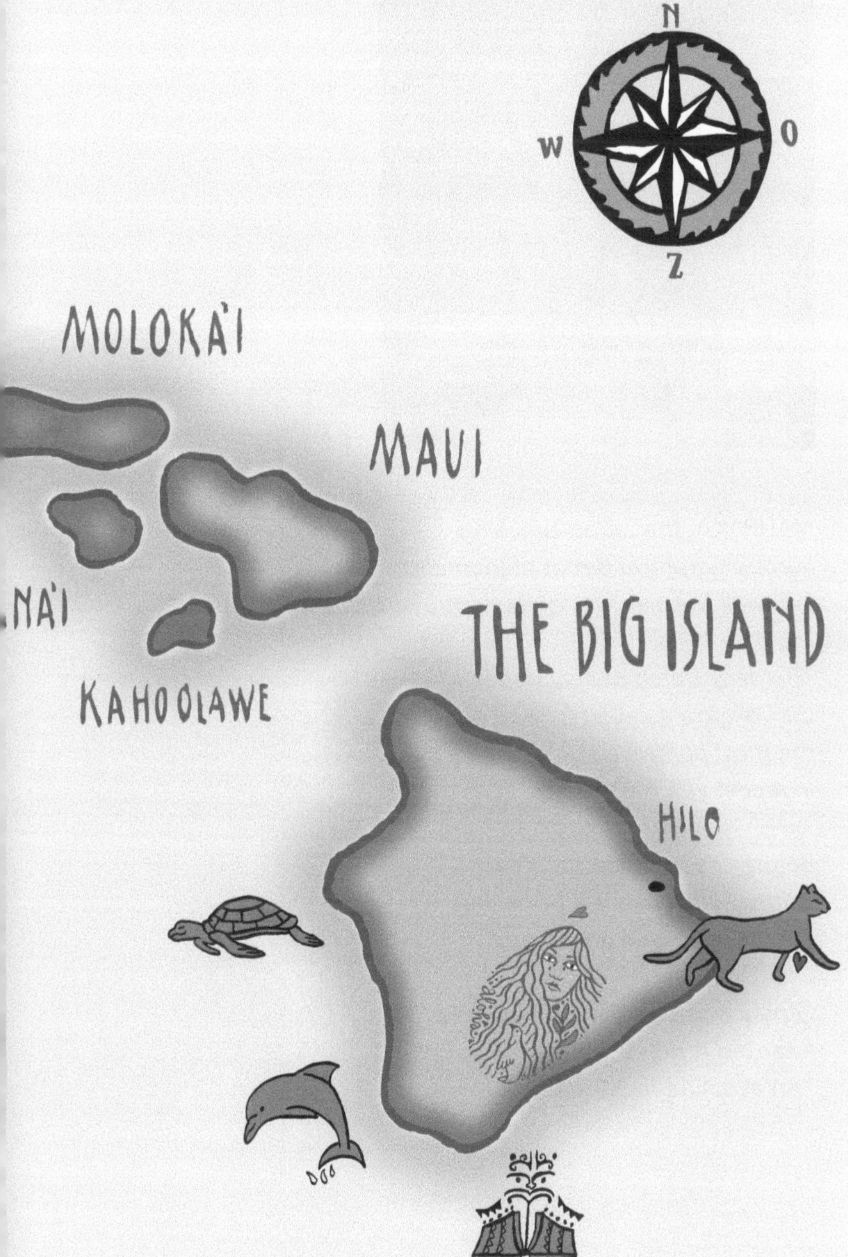
N
W
O
Z
MOLOKA'I
MAUI
NA'I
KAHOOLAWE
THE BIG ISLAND
HILO

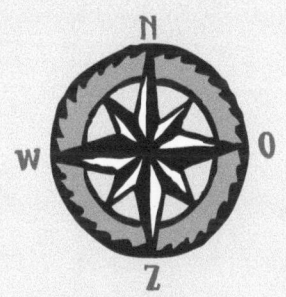

NAUPAKA, the taboo-breaking
autobiographical debut of journalist
Lideweij Bosman was quite controversial.

The daily Dutch quality paper
De Volkskrant called it "one of
the most controversial books
in recent years".

Belgian news magazine Knack
writes: "Naupaka is a book that
will leave no-one unmoved."

Glossy women's magazine Grazia
awarded it with 5 stars:
"An absolute must-read".

Lideweij is thousands of miles away from her true love, while he is fighting for his life. They'd been inseparable for years, fighting Hodgkin's Lymphoma side by side, until Lideweij makes the excruciating decision not to be at his side when he passes away. She leaves for Hawaii, the place where only ten months earlier Sander had proposed to her and told her about the legend of the naupaka flower.

Her journey helps her to work through the deep sorrow. Tears are gradually replaced by inspiring insights and new dreams.

28 JUNE 2013

@Shendersson, 19:42
"Fighting, almost dead... But not just yet!!!"

Introduction

7306 miles away from me the love of my life is on his deathbed. He, my best friends and even my own mother have begged me to come back. But a deep inner feeling inside me is stronger, and it tells me that I have to stay here. On Hawaii. Close to the woman whose face I see in my dreams. In the same place where he and I walked, barely a year ago...

There he is, at the foot of the bed. Sander, my one and only, standing there, with his buzz cut and stubble. "Li! Shall we go see the sunrise? Or would you rather sleep a little longer?" No need to think twice about that. I swing my legs off the mattress and slip into my favorite pair of silver-gray Havaiana's. Although I prefer to call them "Hawaiana's", as we are in Kaua'i, one of the Hawaiian islands.

"Then we'd better hurry!" Sander is already standing in the doorway of our lodge. He grabs my hand, gives it a brief squeeze and leads me outside. In the garden the white and yellow frangipani flowers are already spreading their delicious, fresh sweet smell. We follow a path, with dense ferns and hibiscus flowers as big as your hand, and end up in a small bay with crystal clear water and a pearly white sandy beach, with one lone crooked palm tree. Little white crabs scurry away from our feet, looking for pools of sea water. I spot a tree trunk with three words carved into the wood: "Angel enlighten one".

"Why don't we cuddle up right here?" I ask, pulling Sander towards me. Silently we stare at the golden orange play

of light on the horizon. After a while Sander turns around and picks a tiny white flower. He carefully places it in the palm of my hand; it's no bigger than the top of my thumb.

"Wow, that's funny, it's a half-flower! It only has petals on the bottom."

Sander nods. "There's an extraordinary legend about this flower. The story took place on the biggest island of Hawaii, on Big Island. A long, long time ago a young couple that was very much in love lived there. But the Fire Goddess of the island, Pele, decided to throw a spanner in the works. She tried to seduce the man, but didn't manage, because his heart belonged to someone else. The goddess was furious. If she could not have him, no one could. She chased him into the mountains and pelted him with lava stones. The Fire Goddess' sisters could not bear the sight and decided to transform him into a half-flower. They named the flower "naupaka", which was the name of the mountain where he'd been sent. Pele's sisters then did the same with his true love."

Sander picks another flower, pressing their hearts close together. "According to the legend they will one day grow back towards each other and become one flower again." He sighs heavily. 'My lovely, lovely Li, the legend of Naupaka is our story, because we are also being torn apart by evil and we will not grow old together either. But I'm sure that we will one day also become one flower again, in whatever form that may be." He gets down on one knee in the sand, takes my hand and asks me, his eyes full of tears: "Will you marry me?" A ray of sun lights up his blue-gray eyes that look up at me expectantly. I lean towards him and kiss him on the lips. "Yes, my love. Yes!"

PART ONE
FIGHTING
THE NETHERLANDS, 2012
OUR LAST YEAR TOGETHER

1   A survival rate of 8%

That's it then. Here I am, with a bowl of scrambled eggs with chia seeds and a cup of strong tea in front of me, sitting in our ground-floor flat of 700 square feet in the northern borough of Utrecht.

"It's going to be a rainy week," says the weather man on the morning news. The spring is showing its dark side. Just like me, because I've been home from work since a few weeks. "A burnout," said my GP. I prefer to call it "stressed-out", which sounds a lot less official and not quite as serious.

I fill my days with boring household chores like vacuuming and mopping. The living room, kitchen and bathroom have never been so spick-and-span. And although my own spring feeling is still buried somewhere deep inside, our small city garden is a dazzling display of daffodils and crocuses and hyacinths. The first day of spring, a few weeks ago, was pure torture. Everyone was out enjoying the sun, while we were stuck inside; Sander had just had another grueling round of chemotherapy.

I was actually annoyed with the people barbecuing in the park, annoyed with the overflowing side walk terraces. I wasn't allowed to join in but I could see it right there, the life my heart so yearned for. Why did this have to happen to us? I too wanted the white picket fence-life. While all our friends are getting pregnant, having great careers and are able to buy their dream house, we've been battling cancer for four years straight now.

I'm hardly sick, not like Sander is, but I'm so battle-weary.

My remedy? Meditation, mindfulness exercises, pure chocolate, relaxing in the sauna, jogging in green surroundings, retail therapy and lunch dates with girlfriends.

Not working, but doing fun stuff; it feels kind of ambivalent. And yet I have to let go of these emotions, just like I will have to try to forget my fears for the future; otherwise I will end up going over the cliff's edge all the same.

A few weeks ago Sander's very last medical trump card – Lenalidomine, officially intended as a treatment for bone cancer, but in some cases it also seemed to work against Hodgkin's Lymphoma - was overtrumped. He now has a measly eight percent survival rate. I feel a knot in my stomach when I remember what the internist told us: a survival rate of less than ten percent. It's hopeless; things are not going to work out.

And ever since, I've done nothing but worry. It feels like I'm drowning in my own whirlpool of thoughts and doubts. Will I ever be able to laugh again? And I mean really laugh. Will I ever be able sit on a side walk terrace again without a worry in the world? Will I ever dare to contemplate the future again? And what will a future without Sander look like? In order to not drive myself completely crazy, I repeat the following mantra over and over: *"Sander is not going to die. Sander is not going to die."* But I don't sound all that convinced. Where is the battle-spirit I used to have four years ago?

> *The metro has just passed the Duivendrecht train station when my phone rings. "It's not good, Li." Sander sounds very calm. "They want me to go to hospital and get some scans right away." There's a ringing sound in my ears. This past year he'd been suffering from all kinds of weird symptoms: inexplicable itching, terrible sweats at night, and he was extremely tired. He would suddenly fall asleep: in the car, on the couch, during a dinner with my family. My brother*

was worried and had at one point asked me if Sander was perhaps doing drugs. Because his eyes and cheeks were so hollow, his body was gaunt, and his skin was ashen. The GP had not known what to make of it and came to the conclusion that the high inflammatory markers in his blood were the cause of the many scratch wounds on his skin. Just to be sure she referred him to an orthomolecular doctor, whose guess was as good as hers, and who advised him to "leave out the sugar for now". Sander dutifully obeyed. The result? He lost even more weight. Or at least, that's what we thought. When all of a sudden a big bump appeared in his neck, it turned out that all his symptoms were traceable to Hodgkin's Lymphoma, or "Hodgkin's", as most Dutch people call it in the vernacular. The assassin had quietly been able to work himself up to an advanced grade four.

However, we were relieved when the internist told us that the treatment resulted in a survival rate of no less than ninety percent. Hodgkin's is the oldest and considered to be one of the most curable forms of cancer. Sander's first chemo worked like a charm. He suffered little side-effects and felt great. His life force returned and within a few months back was the guy I'd fallen head over heels in love with. The following months were a dream. We partied, went to loads of dance festivals, splurged all our money on vacations and laughed like nothing had ever happened. "We're not going to give up," was Sander's new life motto. And: "I've got Hodgkin's, but Hodgkin's doesn't have us."

But then, on Christmas Eve of all nights, a scan revealed several new tumors, and they were growing. That really was a wake-up call. This was not just any disease, this was cancer. And you can die from cancer.

I force myself to stop worrying, take out my iPhone and scroll through my list of contacts, in search of someone to have lunch with. But who? Everyone is either at work or busy with the kids. Maybe Juuls, who works as a freelance journalist. I bet she'll have time. She picks up after the second ring. "Hey, Li!" her high-spirited voice greets me. "You want to meet up in town? I'd love to. See you there in an hour, okay?" *My lifesaver. Hooray for self-employment!*

Two hours later, with a much lighter heart, two bags full of new comfort clothes and a wet umbrella, I take bus 38 to Utrecht-North. Just when I want to check in with my travel card, the bus suddenly accelerates and I end up tripping over someone's foot. A guy grabs me by the arm and makes sure I don't fall. "Thanks", I mumble. Two friendly eyes peer at me from under a green/white baseball cap.

"I guess the bus driver is sidelining as a matchmaker," he winks at me. I flush, smile sheepishly and walk to a seat all the way in the back of the bus. Am I allowed to flirt, despite my steady relationship of no less than twelve years? I'm instantly overcome with shame. My boyfriend is extremely ill and here I am wondering if flirting is allowed! Sander is my buddy and I'm still very much in love with him. But I also know I could lose him any moment. Four years of taking care of him have left me worn-out and my fears of what the future will bring are getting worse and worse. In a while Sander might not be here anymore. What then? Will I ever meet a new true love? But won't I then be too old to have children?

It's almost dark when I get off the bus. In the highest tree in our street a blackbird sings its evening song. I pause to listen when I hear a car approach. The bird is overruled by the *thump, thump* of a loud house beat. *Wait, I know that song,* and as soon as I turn around, I see it's Sander behind the steering wheel, with a big grin on his face while his right hand is tapping along with the beat. He rolls down the window and whistles at me. "Hey there, gorgeous!" he shouts, loud enough so the whole street can hear him. A man sitting on the terrace in front of the restaurant on the corner turns to us with a smile. He lifts up his beer. "Cheers mate, I'll drink to that!"

I get in the car and plant a kiss on his lips while I take in the spicy smell of Chanel on his warm skin. "Hi there, sweetie! How was work?"

"Great!" He sounds positively radiant. "Actually, it was really great! I can't really figure it out, but without those pepper-uppers like Prednison and Dexamethasone I actually feel pretty good. But I guess we'd better wait and see how the rest of the week goes." He tucks a lock of blond hair behind my ear. Sander is feeling good and wants to continue taking part in normal life as long as possible. His work at the television production company is a good distraction.

"Hey, why don't we grab a pizza in town? And uh... we could just go by car, because you're not allowed to drink anyway," I add with a mischievous wink. Because if there's anyone who likes a stiff drink, it's Sander. Before he started with this new medication, he would drink two bottles of wine a day, and good wine too, in order to avoid a hangover. But alcohol is a definite no-no during this treatment.

"You've got to believe me," he'd announced solemnly when I'd asked him if he would ever stop drinking. "I promise that once I start on this medication, everything will change," he'd said, waving his glass of Pouilly-Fussé at me. "From that moment onwards, I can and will face the battle."

A moment later he suddenly turns down the volume of the car radio. "Actually, I am a bit tired. Shall we just order in some sushi and watch *Breaking Bad?*" The series is about a chemistry teacher with lung cancer who starts to manufacture and sell drugs to ensure his family will have enough money once he's gone. "Who knows, I might even learn a thing or two so that you can go on a shopping spree in the P.C. Hoofstraat," he adds with a twinkle in his eyes.

When I get out of the car, the neighbor's cat saunters over. She's brown-black with a white spot on her nose and she greets me with a soft head butt and a lot of loud meowing.

"Hey there, Miss Alley Cat," Sander cries out. "And how are you doing today?" She quickly goes up to him and snakes around his legs. As soon as we open the door to our apartment the smell of peonies hits me. Because of the heat of the gas fire, the huge flowers have burst open and turned into veritable perfume bombs. I walk up to the table and take a flower out of the large glass vase.

"Sweetie, come and smell this!" Sander leans in towards the anthers and takes a big whiff. "Amazing!" he cries out, embracing me. "You know that I really love that about you, that you can enjoy little things like this. I'm so glad that you passed that on to me."

I freeze in his arms. He just used the past tense. *Is he saying goodbye?* I feel a panic attack coming on.

"What's wrong?" Sander sounds upset.

Shall I tell him what I was thinking? I know how important it is to share things, however confronting it may be.

Sander pulls me towards him and continues in an upbeat tone of voice: "I really want to learn many more plant and tree names from you, because I still know so few of them. Like cowslip, those are the big yellow flowers by the water, and not the little ones in our garden, right?" He's pointing at the pilewort that's growing rank. He kisses me; I feel his lower lip trembling slightly, a sure sign that he's not as upbeat as he sounds.

"You know what I was thinking, didn't you?" I ask, tentatively.

Sander nods. "Of course. You and me, we've got a very

strong connection, girl."

We order sushi for four at the best Japanese restaurant in town and settle down in the comfy cushions on the couch. Sander puts his feet on my lap and turns to me with his pitiful doggy eye look. "Would you please give me a foot massage?" I take off his black sport socks and touch the dark blue veins on top of his feet. They not only contained many liters of chemotherapy, but also the experimental drug sgn-35. This new form of therapy would go straight to the disease instead of also destroying all the healthy body cells, or at least that's what the patient information leaflet said. After only a few administrations, Sander did indeed make a miraculous recovery and seemed disease-free. Except that the medication also caused permanent damage to his nervous system, with numb feet and finger tips as a result. They cut the treatment short to prevent further paralysis.

Sander soon falls into a deep sleep and his face becomes shroud-like white. I know that I don't need to worry but it still looks scary. As if his illness is momentarily revealing itself to me. Sander, my handsome guy with his buzz cut and stubble. He used to spend hours in front of the mirror, fixing his hair, until he had to shave it off right before chemo. However, his new haircut looked great and ever since the clipper is doing overtime.

That night we both sleep restlessly and bump into each other twice in the bathroom. Around five o'clock in the morning I'm wide awake. I stare out the bedroom window, where I slowly see the contours of our garden shed becoming more distinct. The neighbor's cat that suddenly jumps over the fence onto our driftwood garden table startles me. My heart is doing overtime. I stay in bed and try to calm down by quietly meditating. Usually I manage to reach a state of deep relaxation within minutes, but this time the thoughts take over. *How long will this next treatment take? Maybe Sander will stay sick for God knows how many years and we will never have children. What if I lose my job because I'm no longer able to function properly? Then we will have no more money for fancy dinners and city breaks, the only things that still add a bit of fun to our life.* The panic is getting worse and worse. We will never get through this. Oh my God, we will never get through this!!

"God, if you exist, please help me," I cry out softly towards the ceiling. "If life really has nothing more to offer, then let me just die as well." Nothing happens. Total silence, except for Sander's breathing. But now I'm feeling anger. "Dammit, just give me a sign that you exist!" And then, on the left side of the bed, a green haze appears. Scared I pull the duvet over my eyes. I carefully fold it back a little and see how the light becomes brighter and brighter and then starts to emit a series of small electrical currents towards the side of the bed. Funny enough I'm no longer scared; on the contrary, a wave of love sweeps over me. It's so hot that I break out into a sweat. Awestruck, I whisper: "I'm not sure who or what you are, but please, help me. It's so incredibly difficult to live with this fear. I don't want to lose Sander."

The green apparition takes on a long rectangular shape and stands there, motionless, next to the bed, without a human expression or any form of communication. When I try to focus on the light, my eyelids suddenly feel very heavy and I fall into a deep sleep.

Beams of sunlight peek through a crack in the bedroom curtains. A loud bell clangs through the neighborhood, children's voices echo over the playground outside the school next to our garden. Eight o'clock, time to get up. The mattress next to me is empty. Sander is already in the shower and is loudly singing a song he made up himself, using my nickname, "Liedje", which means "little song" in Dutch. It always makes me smile when he sings this. "Liedje, a happy little melody, a girl who always smiles." It's incredibly cute and adorable, but he's singing it so awfully loud that everyone in our street can hear it, whether they want to or not.

"Good morning, sweetie pie!" I squeeze in next to him under the pathetic weak flow of water and pull him close to me. We stay like that for a while, tightly wrapped in each other's arms.

"Today is the beginning of a new phase. Full of love, happiness and miracles," I say quietly. I decide to keep the wondrous nightly apparition to myself for now.

2 Going out of your mind

Laid out on the bedroom floor are two outfits. I don't know which one to wear. The sights are set high, because Sander is the deejay tonight and I have to be the shining star at his side. Just the thought of standing on the dance floor in a few hours is enough to send a surge of adrenalin through my whole body. I'm desperate for some uplifting beats and sweet rum coke cocktails. I look in the mirror and make a full turn. And another. *Hmm, not bad.* I decide to prepare myself a healthy meal first as a good solid base for a wonderful evening.

Soon after I hear a beat from the living room; Sander is preparing his set for tonight. "Wow! Nice outfit!" he manages to shout, despite the ear splitting techno beat. "Good thing you're coming to my party tonight. I'd better keep an eye on you." We do a little dance in the living room. I wrap my arms around his waist, kissing him on his soft lips and prickly chin. In his eyes I can see he's tired. "Are you sure you're okay?" I ask, slightly ill at ease. "Are you really up to a whole night of playing?"

He walks to the cupboard and takes out a small tray with pills. "Why don't I treat myself to some Dexamethasone, a little pepper-upper from the hospital. It's not as if I don't take any pills, right."

Club Moira is in the center of Utrecht. At first glance you wouldn't think that there's a dance venue right in the middle of a neat row of white townhouses, but a hidden staircase leads to a large hall.

"Let's go and sit down over there," says Juuls, an old friend from school, pointing towards the benches against the wall. "I just happen to have brought us a special treat."

I immediately know what she's talking about. *Candy. Pills. Ecstasy.* She takes a transparent bag out of her purse and presses it into my hand. "You go to the restrooms first." My heart is thumping in my chest. It's been a while since I last took one of these and I still find it exciting. How will my body react? Will it be a pill that makes you float in the air and makes you all introvert? Or one that makes you brash and lively, so that you end up talking to strangers for hours on end as if you're the best of friends? "Pill prattle" is what Sander sometimes calls it.

I feel slightly guilty. Here I am, in a rank toilet cubicle with a pink pill between my fingertips. "Fuck it. Tonight I'm going all out. I'm gonna go off the deep end, 'cause who knows how near the end is anyway." I nibble at a corner of the little pill and instantly recognize the bitter taste. I down the last bit with a big gulp of water. "Bring it on," I shout at my own reflection in the mirror. I fix my bangs, tie my bleached white hair back in a pony-tail, purse my lips and apply a thick layer of Yves Saint Laurent lipstick, leaving the imprint of a kiss on my own reflection.

"Oh yes, I'm definitely feeling it," says Juuls, rolling onto her left side, with her head on a red velvet pillow. "Do you already feel something?"

"Yeah, I feel quite a lot," I answer in a low voice. In my stomach an adrenaline-like force is slowly spreading towards my arms. "Shall we go and dance?"

"Hmm... I think I'd rather just lie here for a little bit longer, okay?" She closes her eyes and surrenders herself to the pink pill that is taking her to higher spheres, far away from Moira, from Utrecht, from Holland, from the Earth. I find it more difficult to let go. I feel restless. Maybe I should go and pee? Or a piece of gum, that might also do the trick. But where is Sander? I know he had some on him. Is he already playing his set? No, I haven't seen him yet. He won't be on for another hour. I stare into the half empty space in front of me. I miss him. Where is he? I feel fear creeping up on me.

"Juuls! I'm gonna go for a walk!" She opens her eyes, startled. "My gosh, I'm really tripping out," she mumbles. "Jeez, these pills are strong! Let's dance!"

Arm in arm, we fly over the dance floor.

"Hottie at three o'clock, over by the coats," Juuls shouts. I turn around and see him, dressed in a short black leather coat, a white T-shirt with a deep V-neck, and a dark brown bag slung over his shoulder. I hurry over as quickly as possible. "Hello there, Mister Ep." That's Sander's deejay alias. He turns around and flashes me a wide grin. I hang on to his neck and take in his warm smell: a mix of fresh evening air, tobacco and Chanel. He looks at me with a knowing smile. "Ah, Liedje, are you maybe going a tiny bit wild? Go ahead and enjoy it."

"Yeah. But it's okay, right?" I look at him expectantly.

"Have you got anything left for later?"

"I'll ask Juuls. But first you'd better go and give us a good house set so that we can loosen up a little." He pinches my bum and walks towards the stage to install his gear.

The dark, smoky dance floor is by now as crowded as can be. And there is my love, headphones halfway around his ears, his hands on the buttons. He looks at the dance floor and turns down the volume. Someone whistles encouragingly. All eyes are on Sander. And then, with one twist of his hand, he throws us a deafening beat. Hands go up in the air; people are yelling and jumping up and down. Sander takes his hands off the turntable, gets up and looks into the crowd. I try to make my way over, pushing sweaty bodies out of the way.

"Jeez, that deejay is hot," I overhear a girl say. I look up, searching for Sander, and see he's moving along with the crowd. He loves this. This is his big dream. To send the crowd into ecstasy with his music. Our eyes find each other, he blows me a kiss. He mouths "I love you".

A girl glances at me with question marks in her eyes. "Is that your boyfriend?! You lucky girl!" If only she knew. This might be his last deejay performance ever.

3   Wanting a child

"Maybe we should think about having a baby," says Sander after an evening stroll on the beach near Bloemendaal aan Zee. "Would you want that?"

"*Could* you!?" I throw him a frightened look. "With the future as uncertain as it is now?"

Sander stares at the turbulent gray water for a second or two, where sea gulls perform ultra quick air raids on tiny fish.

"Let's just find out what the options are," he suggests. "Wouldn't it be great to have a little lady or a tiny man and be a real family?"

In a flash I see a vision of that future: a miniature version of Sander is running through the garden of our dollhouse near the river Vecht, being chased by the greatest dad in the world and a fluffy cute mongrel called "Little Mister". Sander notices the soft smile that makes the corners of my mouth go up. "That would really be wonderful, wouldn't it? Why don't we think of a boy's and a girl's name? What about 'Dex'?" He rattles on. "Hmm, on second thought, maybe not. That sounds like an abbreviation for Dexamethasone." He throws me a momentary look full of doubt, but he collects himself after a few seconds. "What about a girl?'

"Elin," is my immediate reaction, explaining my choice: "It sounds both cute and tough."

The unrest that I've been trying to repress is brought to the surface by the roaring waves. "But what if I end up with a toddler all on my own? It's not as if our parents live next door to help me out."

"Then you move to Haarlem. Then you'll have friends and my family close by."

I slowly let myself warm to the idea, glad for every ray of hope or possible solution. "Okay, let's look into the possibilities."

Me *not* wanting a baby, that's out of the question. I would love to be a mother, but the chances that Sander and I manage to conceive a child are quite slim. Due to all the treatments Sander is now infertile, so the only possibility would be IVF with Sander's banked sperm, something that the doctors advised us to do before he started with chemo.

"So you've come to deliver some sperm then?" the receptionist asks. I almost feel caught in the act when she turns to me. "Would you like to accompany him?" I try to pull a deadpan face when I respond. "Sure, why not." She points us towards a hallway with five doors. "Just pick a room, any room." Sander gingerly opens the first door and peers inside. "Just imagine walking in on someone. Now there's a comforting thought," he whispers nervously.

'Where's the light switch, San?" I ask. "It's so dark here."

"It might be a dark room," he jokes. I playfully hit him on the arm. "Hey, didn't you like my pun, Li?"

I switch on the light. On the left side of the room I see a simple folding chair, next to it a box of tissues and a dust bin. On the right are shelves with two neat piles of magazines and several DVD's. Sander immediately heads that way. "The Playboy and Penthouse!" He's all eyes now, taking the top magazine off the shelf and leafing through it.

I glance at the platinum blondes with oversized lips and breasts. "Jeez, just what you'd expect," I mutter. "Not a wrinkle in sight and plenty of inflated boobs and butts. How can a University Hospital dish up bodies that have undergone unnecessary cosmetic surgery? It's disgusting."

Sander looks at me and caresses my cheek with the back of his hand. "Sweetie, the idea is that you get me wound up, not yourself."

I switch on the television and continue in a more serious tone of voice: "Okay then sir, if you would please remove your clothes while I turn on this educational film about your treatment."

He frowns, followed by a deep sigh. "Nice try, Li, but I don't think that's going to work."

Slightly disappointed, I decide I'd better leave. "Don't worry, it's a romantic movie,' I say, giving him an understanding kiss, "with a happy end."

Four years later I find myself back in the same hospital ward, anxiously looking at the roll of stomach fat in my left hand and the sharp needle in my right. Yes or no? I'm here because I have to learn how to inject myself with hormones in preparation of the ivf treatment because we've decided that we do want to try to get pregnant. But it's not quite as simple as that. We had to appear before a board of social workers and psychologists, to defend our desire to have a child. "Will you be able to handle a baby, with all the uncertainty in your life you already have to deal with?" they asked us.

"But of course!" Sander had answered forcefully. "In fact, we've become an incredibly close-knit team *because* of my illness." A week later they gave us the green light.

"You won't feel a thing, don't worry," a nurse in his mid-twenties with a blond crew cut and chubby upper arms and butt reassures me. There are three other women sitting around the round table, *with* their partners. One of the men – stocky, with a tribal tattoo on his left forearm – looks away the moment his brunette plants the needle in her stomach with one swift movement. *Wussy.*

Meanwhile I'm sitting there all by myself, with the knowledge that the chance of Sander dying (92%) is higher than the chance of me getting pregnant (25%). Although we've been over the worst case scenario dozens of times, and I try to draw faith from the idea that my friends and family would help me out should Sander not be able to anymore, I'm still wrecked by doubts. Am I not frantically holding on to the vision of a future that's just not meant for us? I return the needle to the tray in front of me. *No, I simply cannot create new life on a foundation of fear and uncertainty.* I get up, take my coat from the coat rack and quickly walk to the exit. In the car, on my way home, I worry about how to break the news to Sander. I feel guilty, as if I'm giving up now that I know he is not going to make it.

4   A spiritual search

It's almost as if I work through my fears at night. My dreams have been rather exciting, especially these past few weeks. I write them down the moment I wake up, and not because they're so absurd, but because of the hidden messages they contain.

And something strange is happening: a remarkable number of dreams have come true. I've seen five good friends have a baby, and that's just one example. This experience is new to me. I want to explain the inexplicable but I soon discover that the rational journalist I have become does not stand a chance in Wonderland. The only thing I *can* conclude is that these intense emotions of terror and despair have stripped my protective layer to the core, and ever since I seem to be susceptible to undefined energies.

The ambition to develop myself as a journalist turns into a longing to investigate new things; to follow a spiritual path, to embark on a journey towards inner blossoming. Maybe I can find a different way to heal Sander now that all the conventional medical treatments no longer seem to work?

For myself this results in a healthier diet, jogging, and daily meditation sessions. I even take a Reiki course: a Japanese form of energetic healing that restores harmony in the body's meridians and chakra's. The effect is quite astonishing. One day I lay my hands on Sander's weary body - which after a particularly tough round of chemo, refuses to hold any food or liquid - and after twenty minutes he suddenly gets up with a big smile on his face and asks me what I would like to eat, "'cause then I'll go get us some groceries".

I want to explore everything that spontaneously crosses my path and during this spiritual quest one of the things I delve into is the history of natural religions and witchcraft. I start burning white sage to purify the rooms in our house and to cleanse myself from daily worries. I also learn a little trick to protect myself from energy absorbing people and situations: by visualizing a silver dome around my body. Another visualization that I practice daily is picturing a thread that runs from my tailbone into the ground and firmly embeds me in the red-hot core of the earth. It helps you to stay in your power, to ground. And after a few weeks of practice I come to the conclusion that it really works. Deadlines and meetings are no longer as exhausting as they were. I feel more energetic, happier.

I start performing these rituals in the garden, rather than in the house. I burn little pieces of paper at full moon, on which I've written wishes or elements of my life that I want to release.

"My sexy little witchy," Sander calls me half-mockingly. But he doesn't dare to get his fingers burnt on my witchcraft.

"I think I'm going to burn you at the stake," he says one evening when I'm outside in the garden again.

"Haha! You'll never manage, not once I've turned you into a frog," I shriek, adding a witch-like cackle for extra effect.

One day I come home from work and catch Sander burning sage in the living room. Even though he never consciously immerses himself in things that go beyond his reasoning, he has become more and more curious about the intangible things in life. During a scan he has a spiritual experience. "I saw an eagle flying over me and then suddenly I was the one soaring over mountain tops and looking down at the Earth."

Soon after I discover that angels can make their presence known to us humans through tiny flashes of light or colorful pulsating energy. That's exactly what happened in the bedroom the other night! When I share this with my mother she tells me that I used to see colors as a toddler. I decide I want to find out more about these divine creatures. Take the archangels, of which there are several, like the powerful healer Raphael and the protector Michael. Apparently you can always ask them for help, no matter the time of day and whatever kind of difficulty you're struggling with. They can relieve both pain and emotions. If you see little feathers on the street or remarkable digital combinations on clocks, such as 11:11, it's them letting you know they're nearby.

But while I'm diligently looking for alternative healing techniques, Sander is well on his way to a self-destructive path and increasingly reaching for the bottle. Alcohol is the only way he is able to forget his fear of dying and to numb the ever worsening symptoms, especially the itching. My frenetic endeavors to try and save him now only seem to irritate him. When one afternoon I want to give him Reiki and he doesn't want me to, we get into a huge argument.

"But I'm only trying to help you!" I'm fuming.

He gives a dismissive wave as if my words mean nothing to him. "I just don't believe that stuff. Do you really think you can cure me with all those spiritual things? No, Lide. The only thing that could have helped me was chemo. It's just tough luck for me."

5 Blessed Christmas

Bzzzzzzzzzzzt, bzzzzzzzzzzt goes the snooze of our alarm clock. Soft but insistent. We have to get up, there's no escaping this. But today we really, really don't want to get up. Because today they're going to tell us the results of a scan that will show how quickly the disease is spreading now that Sander's treatment has ended. To put off the torturous journey to the hospital just a little longer we snuggle up against each other. I know how badly Sander likes to avoid doctor's appointments. And it is inhumane that they make you wait for minutes on end for a result that will determine if it's life or death. If only we could run away, and fast. But we can't outrun this result. I still remember Christmas Eve four years ago very vividly.

Even though it's Christmas Eve, the Hematology Ward is bustling with activity, contrary to the rest of the hospital, where the hallways and waiting rooms are deserted. While everyone is preparing for the merriest and coziest night of the year, we're terrified because we're about to get Sander's scan results.

Is the disease back? Sander is staring straight ahead with a glazed look in his eyes. Our eyes are focused on the door of the doctor's office. My heart skips a beat every time the door opens and our doctor appears. We attempt to read the verdict from the look on the hematologist's face.

"This is bad, I just know it," Sanders says when the doctor

appears again. "We'd better prepare for the worst, Liedje".
When I hear those words I slowly sink into a swirling tur-
moil of fear. Colors fade and the voices around me become
fainter and fainter.

"Mr. Ebbeling?" The doctor's voice brings me back to the
here and now. And it turns out Sander's feeling was right.

"Despite the chemotherapy we're seeing a manifestation
of the disease. The only possible treatment is an autologous
stem cell transplant." His words feel like axe blows. "It's a
drastic procedure, with a significant risk of death."

He explains that high-dose chemotherapy will destroy
Sander's immune system and thereby, hopefully, also destroy
the "roots" of the tumors. The idea is that the blood cells of
Sander's own stem cells – that will be harvested a few weeks
prior via a central line in his groin, filtered from his blood
and subsequently frozen – will start to grow again and reac-
tivate his immune system. Without this drastic procedure he
will surely die, that much is clear. The sessions will take three
weeks, with a recovery period of several months to half a
year. Ten minutes later, shell-shocked by the news, we're back
in the car on our way to a crappy Christmas.

We're still lying in bed when all of a sudden Sander's arm
starts to shake. "Hey, look, that's weird." Surprised, he points
to his right arm that has started shaking uncontrollably from
his shoulder all the way to his fingers. "I'm dying!" he screams
in full-blown panic. "This is it!"

I grab his arm. "Come on, sweetie. Let's go take a shower.
A splash of water will sort you out." I sound a lot calmer
than I'm feeling. But we don't even make it to the shower.
Right before the sink, Sander collapses. His body slides down
the white bathroom tiles and hits the cold floor. Motionless,
crooked, with his chin on his chest, he just lies there. I break

into a cold sweat. *"Sander!"* I shout. "Stay with me! Wake up!" I try to get him to sit up, so that he can at least get some air. *Is he still breathing?* A thin thread of saliva seeps out of the left corner of his mouth. From underneath his boxer shorts feces are dripping onto the black and white checkered linoleum.

"No! *No!*" I yell. My voice sounds terribly high-pitched. *Doesn't that happen to people who are dying?* My hands are trembling while I fumble to unlock my mobile to call 911. A calm woman's voice answers.

"You've got to help us!" I scream in a rush of total panic. "You have to come right away." And then we get disconnected. I quickly grab the sink, because I'm about to pass out myself now. When I manage to call her back, the woman tells me that the ambulance is already on its way. I run to the front door to open it and then run back to Sander, who is slowly regaining consciousness. He stares around him like a lifeless being and attempts to stand up like a newborn foal, but his knees buckle every time.

And then he suddenly gets a terrified look on his face. This is not the Sander I know. "Bathroom," he mumbles, pushing me aside with an unbelievable force. I trip and bump my arm. He regards me with the look of a predator, stumbles towards the living room and collapses on the sofa. Soon after I see a blue flashing light behind the curtains and a few seconds later two women and two men appear, clad in fluorescent yellow visibility jackets. One of the paramedics kneels down next to Sander. "How are you feeling, sir?"

"Fine," he answers, as if nothing happened. My jaw drops. And just like that, Sander is back. As if nothing happened! Silent tears of relief run down my cheeks. Within a few minutes they've hooked him up to all kinds of monitors. One of the paramedics gives us the run-down: "His heart rate is too high with 140 beats per minute and his oxygen level is too low."

Sander is slowly recovering and turns to me. "Sweetie! You look so frightened! Are you okay?"

I want to tell him everything, I want to cry, I want to throw myself in his arms and be comforted, but I have to stay strong. "I'm fine and everything is gonna be okay, babe. I'm going fetch you some things now, because we have to go to hospital."

The rest of the day at the Utrecht University Hospital is devoted to blood tests and scans. At some point, like an aftershock after an earthquake, Sander's arm starts to shake again.

"Go fetch help. *Quick!* It's that same feeling again!"

"Help! Someone help us!" I yell, running to the hallway. Nurses appear out of seemingly nowhere and rush towards his room. The hematologist comes in with a big needle on a tray.

"It's epilepsy," he explains. Sander relaxes immediately after the injection. "It's probably due to low blood magnesium levels."

But the truth is quite another matter, as we find out later that evening from the doctor on duty. The tall man, in his mid-thirties, with dark curly hair, kneels down next to Sander's bed. "It's very rare with Hodgkin's Lymphoma, but we've found something in your head. It's small and will probably respond well to radiation."

Our life is at an absolute low point. We spend Christmas at the hospital with - I kid you not - Mrs. Angel and Mr. Bethlehem in the rooms next to ours. I'm even allowed to sleep in Sander's room, which is very exceptional, and the nurses go out of their way to make our Christmas as nice as possible. Among other things this includes fresh orange juice, an egg, and Christmas Stollen for breakfast every morning. Sander's best friend Jorn spends an extremely long evening and night in his kitchen to prepare us an unforgettable Christmas dinner. We eat duck meat rolls, grilled pieces of rib-eye, lemon risotto with Parmesan, Thai curry with tender chunks of free range chicken, and stewed meat in a rich brown sauce. It's incredibly delicious. Sander's boss brings us a small Christmas tree with white glazing and miniature lights. When we turn it on that night and sit there looking at it, we realize this is one of the most beautiful, most memorable Christmases ever, in the loving embrace of family and friends.

Deep in our hearts we also know it will be our last Christmas together. The day before New Year's Eve Sander's fever goes down and we're allowed to go home. At twelve o'clock, when it's time for all the fireworks, we're both in bed, in a deep sleep.

6   Wrecked

Godforsaken, so alone
So, alone. Locked up.

Shackled.
Not able to be together.

Being so godforsaken alone
That's not something you easily break through -
and by yourself it's pointless to wait.

Back to yourself and to that
godforsaken loneliness
to look for new space
for an encounter.

Jeske Alblas

"I can't stand this anymore!" I scream desperately, clawing at the carpet in the bedroom with my fingers. Our battle against cancer has been ongoing for almost four years straight and now that the disease is winning, Sander is drinking himself to death. Alcohol is the only way to soothe the itching for a couple of hours, or so he says. In the past few months I've been finding bottles and cans and glasses absolutely every-where. In the big Chinese vase, behind the bookshelves, in the garden shed, underneath the couch, and in the wardrobe. When I caught Sander drinking on the sly a couple of weeks ago, something snapped.

We're watching a movie. Me with a cup of tea, Sander with a bottle of water. As the evening wears on his coordination deteriorates noticeably. When he trips and knocks over a chair in his fall, I know it's bad news. I pick up the blue water bottle, that's right there in front of me on the oak coffee table, unscrew the cap and smell it.

"Vodka!"

Sander looks at me wide-eyed and reacts forcefully. "No it isn't! It's water! You're paranoid!"

I hesitate for a second. Is he right, have I become paranoid? I feel an intense sadness when I take a sip and taste the sharp burning flavor of alcohol.

"How dare you make me think that I've gone crazy?" I yell. "I can't stand it anymore, the way you're behaving. I hate having to search the house like a policeman to discover where you've been hiding your alcohol."

"So then leave. You know what? Let's just break up! That way you're done with all the other bullshit as well!"

Frustrated I kick the couch on which he's slumped and continue to yell at him, livid with rage. "Ha, finally some wise words." I grab the car keys and slam the door in leaving, causing the windows in the living room to rattle.

"What a bastard," I shout as I take the exit towards the ring road going ninety miles an hour. "How can he do this to me?! I've taken care of his sick body for months, with the healthiest meals and juices and Reiki. And this is my reward?!" My adrenalin level hits a new high when a dazed dove brushes against the window. Sander calls me on my mobile. I refuse to answer and only yell at my iPhone: "Fuck off! Oh no, you know what, just die. You're right, then I would finally be done with all this stupid shit."

"Everything is wrecked. Dammit, it's finished! Our relationship is over." In one sweeping motion I pull a drawer out of the dresser, throw my clothes on the floor and kick the wood until I've smashed the wooden side panels. It doesn't help. "We were soul mates," I sob, sitting there with the white pieces of board stacked like firewood in front of me. "And who am I? What am I worth?" I start yelling, totally freaked out. "Nothing matters anymore. All our dreams are wrecked. Our wedding, our kids, our future, *everything*, gone," I mope in self-pity. "I might as well die since there's no future left anyway."

If only I could have a fit man by my side, with whom I'd live in a beautiful house on the river Vecht, with children playing in the backyard... But what I long for even more is to be able to laugh again, to laugh exuberantly and without a care in the world.

The illness and the alcohol feel like snakes coiling around my neck, tighter and tighter. They're suffocating me. I can't breathe. I lie down on the white carpet and slowly feel myself disappearing into a tunnel of loneliness. And then I suddenly realize Sander is no longer there to help me cope. We can't save each other anymore. The disease is doing us both in.

All is quiet. No tears, no panic, no thoughts. I look around me, bewildered, in search of the last remaining bit of hysterics.

"See. All will be well," I encourage myself. "It's not going to get worse than this. This might actually be the bottom of all fear."

I feel a soft, warm feeling flowing through my body and regain some of my strength; enough to be able to collect some clothes and toiletries. I stuff everything into a big sports bag, get the car keys and call my mother.

"Hi, mom. Is it okay if I come and live with you guys for a while?"

PART 2
LETTING GO
THE NETHERLANDS, 2013
THE YEAR SANDER DIES

7 I have to let you go

A week later we're sitting at our dining table.

"I miss you like crazy, babe," Sander says with a quivering voice, "and I'm so sorry I don't manage to quit drinking. I understand you can't cope with it anymore and I want to give you all the room you need." I look at his whitish hands and wrists that are covered with red scratches. Sander catches me looking. "The itching has been worse than ever these past days, but that's not important now. This is about you and me."

My heart goes out to the man sitting in front of me. *So vulnerable and yet so strong.* It makes my decision all the more difficult, but if I don't do this I will collapse. "I also miss you like crazy, and I'd like nothing more than to lie down next to you with my head on your shoulder. But when I remember how things were, I get so scared."

I sit there swiveling in my chair, trying to keep the tears inside. *Be strong now.*

"It's all jumbled up. I'm confused. And it's driving me crazy."

Sander nods understandingly. "I understand that, Li, and believe me, I'm so, so sorry." He pulls me towards him and wraps his arm around my waist.

"Are you going to get help?" I ask, while he cups my face in his hands.

He gives me a piercing look. "Don't get me wrong, but I'm a bit fed up with all the things I have to do according to others. You, the doctors, my parents. I just can't take it anymore. From now on I'm only listening to me, myself and I. Whether I want to quit, or drink - it has to be my choice. Sorry, Li. I want to be honest with you. I drink because of the terrible despair. I am going to die."

I nod understandingly and know I have to let it go. Let *him* go. He gives me a loving kiss on the forehead, leaving his lips there for a while.

"You're doing great, girlie, don't ever forget that. I'm so proud of you." And then he pushes me towards the couch with a mischievous smile on his lips. "It might not be the right thing to do right now, but what the... Will you please come and lie down next to me for a little while?"

I snuggle up against his body and notice how our breathing soon becomes synchronized. A blanket of peace settles over us, until the itching drives us apart again.

A few days later I'm planting yellow and purple pansies in our little garden while soaking up the first rays of sunshine. Just like the daffodils and crocuses I am also slowly starting to come back into bloom. Sander has temporarily moved in with his parents and it feels really good to be alone for a while, to experience peace and silence within myself. Even though I miss him terribly and I do still feel love for him. So much so that it hurts.

8   Cremation

A few weeks later Sander is sitting next to me again. We're staring at the coffin of my father, who died after heart surgery. I've seen quite a lot of Sander these days and he's been a great support. There's no time to grieve over the end of our relationship; in a few days my father will be cremated and Sander is quite ill due to the radiotherapy sessions for his neck. The tumors were growing so quickly that his airways were at risk and radiotherapy was imperative. Luckily the swelling went down within a few days, but his salivary glands and taste buds have suffered, making it hard for him to swallow. The hair on the right side of his head is falling out. He now wears a cap to hide the bald patches. "At least I won't have to shave that half anymore," is his indifferent reaction to his loss of beard growth.

We paint the white wood coffin with memories of my dad. Sander draws musical notes, in reference to Dire Straits, my father's favorite band, and flowers that symbolize the meadows in the French Provence.

During the cremation we hold hands. Sander suffers from hot flashes and wipes away the beads of sweat on his face with a cotton handkerchief my dad gave him. When I'm no longer able to hold back the tears he dries them lovingly with the same cloth. Our eyes are locked and the eyes of everyone else in the room are focused on the two of us. I know what they're thinking: *When will we be sitting here to say goodbye to Sander?*

The thought alone is sickening.

When he stays over at my place that night we kiss like lovers once again. Waves of green energy pulsate throughout the room. I see them move around us. "Do you see those colors as well, San?" I whisper in his ear.

"That's us, Li. That's our love energy." He lovingly strokes my face and tells me about an extraordinary experience. "Lately I've been seeing a little girl by my bedside. It's not scary or anything, but who do you suppose she is?"

"Maybe she's your guardian angel? I'd cherish her if I were you."

We cuddle up together. I listen to how laborious Sander's breathing has become, a sign that the illness has reached his lungs and throat. I put my hands on his chest and give him Reiki. And again I see colors everywhere. I recall the green apparition I saw a few months ago. "Dear angel, protector or whoever you are, please take away all the pain and fear." When my eyelids grow heavy I wrap myself in a cloak of Sander's love.

9   Memories

One sunny spring day we see each other again and talk about his approaching death. "Will you give me a sign once you're up there, San, so that I'll know there's more between heaven and earth? And to let me know you're okay?"

"If I can, I will certainly do that." He looks at me with weary blue-gray eyes. "But what kind of sign shall I give you?" We sit there in silence, pondering it over, until I say: "It has to be something with music, 'cause that's your passion."

Sander paces around the living room. "I know!" He's elated. "I will suddenly turn on the music, really loud."

He's also thinking about the cremation. "I want a sort of after-party, with lots of booze and my best friends behind the turntable. And everyone has to dance and get drunk." After a short pause he continues, a bit more serious now: "But what I'd really like is for my friends to get together for a copious dinner with greasy chicken and the best red wine while they reminisce about me. Now *that* would be nice."

I'm overcome by a wave of grief. "No San, you can't die," I sob. He gets up and grabs hold of me. "Sweetie! Oh girlie... Come here."

I press myself against him, with my nose against his chest, taking in his warm smell. My senses are acutely aware of everything. My eyes, my ears, my nose; they have to absorb it all so that I don't forget anything.

"I'm okay with this," he says determinedly, holding my face

with both hands. "What kind of life is this, Li? I can't keep this up. The itching is unbearable." He sighs heavily. "I'm so goddamn fed up with all of it."

Wrapped in each other's arms we lie down on the large and comfy couch, like we've been doing for the past thirteen years. But unfortunately Sander can't stay like that for long. "Goddammit," he curses again. "I can't even do this anymore. Due to the warmth of our bodies mine is prickling all over. See, that's what I meant. Life sucks."

We get up and go back to the wooden dining table. "Let's have some wine. It doesn't matter anymore anyway."

Even though my body immediately tenses up because of his proposal, I do go and fetch two crystal wine glasses. I polish them with a cloth until they're all shiny, open a bottle of Chilean red wine and reluctantly hand Sander a glass. It kind of feels like a treacherous act, as if I'm nudging him towards the cliff's edge. Deep within me there's still a glimmer of hope that Sander will miraculously recover and never touch another drink. That we will go back to Hawaii, get married and have lots of kids.

"To us, Li," he brings me back to reality. We toast and spend the rest of the evening thinking back on our lives. Like the first kiss at a college party in *De Harmonie* in Zwolle, The Netherlands. We were both studying journalism at the Hogeschool Windesheim. I was twenty and majoring in Written Press. Sander was twenty-three and majoring in Television & Radio. I had a terrible crush on him, but was crushed that he didn't seem to notice me. Until that evening. After a couple of beers and a tequila I blurted it out: "I kind of like you." Sander didn't say anything for a few seconds, but then took me by the arm and pulled me to a dark corner. "I pretended I wanted to whisper something in your ear, but instead I gave you a surprise kiss," he remembers.

And then we kissed and kissed, until I decided to leave the café. "Why did I leave?" I read his thoughts. "Well, that's pretty obvious!" I throw him an impish look. "I was playing hard to get." That perfect kiss was my trump card. I knew that would work, just like honey attracts bees."

"It's nice to reminisce like this," I continue. "And it probably sounds weird," I whisper, choking up, "but I have the feeling that you will be so ill towards the end that you will no longer be aware of what's happening around you." I start to cry. "Pretty stupid thing to say, right? Sometimes I just don't know anymore *what* I can tell you."

Sander takes my hand in his. "On the contrary, it's really good you're so open and honest. Never, ever feel guilty, okay? You've meant so much to me. Goddamn, this is so difficult." He's also crying. "Liedje, my dear Liedje, never ever forget that you did right. You couldn't have done this any better."

10   Lobi

Sander:
"I miss you so bad it hurts. I'm doing all the things we're
so good at together: exploring towns, browsing mar-
kets and drinking espresso's in hip coffee bars. Why
am I alone?"

Li:

APRIL 6, 2013

Li:

"You're so sweet and I love you so, so much."

Sander:
"I'm a failure, babe. Sometimes I do good.
But more often than not I'm a loser."

Li:

"Peppered with goodness and interlaced
with some raw pieces."

Sander:
"And a hefty dose of *'fail-ness'* on the inside.

Li:

"You mean baldness on the outside?"

Sander:
"Haha, lobi. Dammit, sweetie. I miss you."

11 Hanalei Bay's angel

Sanne is a woman my age, with long, wavy blond hair. She also happens to be the new editor in chief at the fashion magazine where I work. She's passionate, ambitious and quite a tough cookie; those are the keywords that describe her. Like a whirlwind she's brought a much needed breath of fresh air to the editorial staff. She urges us to come up with ideas for new features, to go to fashion events, and to analyze our own work. That's not exactly easy, and it's something I can't muster up the energy for anymore. When the publisher calls me to her office, I smell a rat. She's not going to fire me, is she?

"As you've been absent too many times you don't qualify for your annual raise in salary," she begins, gingerly. "Moreover, we're a bit at a loss what to do with your personal situation," she continues. "The unstable situation at home is impacting on the editorial staff and the continuity of the production cycle."

I knew this talk that has been postponed several times due to sudden hospital admissions was going to come around sooner or later. Now that the moment has come I let out a deep sigh.

These past five years my employer has been incredibly understanding and flexible. The owners, the publisher and the editor in chief all sympathized with Sander and me. Right before his stem cell therapy they even treated us to a weekend getaway in Ameland, an island off the north coast of the country, and they not only paid for the whole thing, but even included a crossing by speed boat instead of the regular ferry.

Now that the publisher is letting me know the party is over, I suddenly realize it's mutual. *What if I decide to stop with the only thing that is preventing me from changing direction?* And right there and then I decide to hand in my notice. It's something I've been considering for a while. But there was always that little voice inside my head warning me that with the recession and all, I would never find another job. After all, my current job offers me financial security in my otherwise so very insecure life.

And before my boss can continue with whatever she wants to tell me, I say, resolutely: "Sorry to interrupt you, but I think I want to quit. I need a fresh start."

She looks up at me with a surprised look on her face. "Really? What a courageous decision. Let's discuss the details later, shall we?"

But what now? It hits me as soon as I've left her office. I could do all kinds of things, but what to choose? I suddenly remember a man Sander and I met on our trip in Hawaii, who taught us all kinds of things about medicinal Hawaiian plants and healing techniques.

> *On one of our last days on the oldest of the Hawaiian islands I finally decide to cross off one of the things on my bucket list: I decide to take a surf lesson. Hanalei Bay is one of the most popular surf spots in the world, surrounded by freakish green mountains and giant waterfalls. Sander looks for a good spot on the beach and sits down among the countless naupaka flowers, while I take my first tentative steps on the surfboard. My instructor is called Elijah and the two hours I spend with him make a huge impression on me. Elijah not only teaches me to surf, he also explains the deeper meaning of it. "To Hawaiians the waves symbolize the flow of life. Only when you can let go of all your thoughts, and trust where*

nature is taking you, will you be able to ride the waves."
After hearing those words of wisdom I manage to take my
first wave without falling. While floating on his longboard, he
tells me about his organic farm and his mission to heal people
through natural techniques. And before I know it I've filled
him in on Sander's medical history. Elijah is dumbstruck.
"Our meeting is no coincidence," he concludes, staring out
over the water. "I'd like to make him a 'blueprint', a plan
specifically targeted for Sander."

Later that afternoon we head for the fruit stand with all
sorts of fresh tropical fruit and juices where Elijah asked us
to meet him. He starts off with the traditional Hawaiian
greeting - a hug and a hefty pat on the back - and motions
us to follow him to his farm, down a winding path flanked
by trees and climbing vines with big purple flowers. There is
an enormous amount of trees with ripe bananas, sweet tart
oranges, and mandarins as large as my fist. Every shrub or
tree possesses healing properties, which Elijah commences to
tell us about. His house stands on top of a hill and is a simple
wooden, sparsely furnished structure. After explaining to us
how superfoods work and how important detoxing is, Elijah
treats Sander to a robust lomi-lomi *massage, a Hawaiian*
technique with deep cleansing and healing properties. Sander's
vertebrae make a snapping sound when Elijah presses down
firmly.
   Before Elijah waves us goodbye an hour later, he quickly
hands Sander a big book with all the knowledge he's been
telling us about and sticks a big red hibiscus flower behind
my left ear.
   "We are now ohana, that's Hawaiian for 'earth family'.
Let the knowledge you now hold uncurl itself like a wave."
   While I watch the man with the baseball cap slowly

disappear in the rearview mirror I realize that meeting this
angel of Hanalei Bay might change the direction of our life.
Maybe his advice can help us overcome Sander's disease?

I decide to look him up on the internet, but I can't find any contact details. When I use the search term "Big Island", "ecological farm" and "healing" I discover a place in the jungle on Big Island where I can learn everything about self-sustained living. Not only how to grow and harvest my own vegetables, fruit and medicinal herbs, but also how to generate solar energy and filter rainwater. It's pretty incredible, there's even a spa. With free use of the gym, Jacuzzi and sauna!

I watch a video where a slender woman tells me what a powerful place it is. "Fire Goddess Pele lives at the top of the mountain and you can definitely feel her energy here."

I stare at the screen, dumbstruck. She's talking about the goddess from the legend of Naupaka, the same goddess that Sander talked about when he proposed to me! It's clear as day; I've got to go there. My eyes slide from the screen to the tattoo of the naupaka flower on my ankle. We both got one made by a well-known tattoo artist on Kaua'i, as a sign of our connection. The sharp pain of the needle on our skin symbolized the emotional pain during all those years of Sander's illness. It was a sort of ritual to find closure for all the pain we'd shared, by reliving the pain together and intensely in this one spot. In a trance of stabbing pain I decided that the half-flower would not only serve as a reminder of my love for Sander but also of the strength within myself.

An hour later I've filled out and sent in the application form. One month later I've got myself a new job at the Hawaiian Sanctuary on Big Island. That job will entail growing and harvesting vegetables and making raw food goodies, plus cleaning the rooms and work areas. In return I will be getting lessons in organic gardening, yoga and meditation. *Oops, wait.* How am I going to tell Sander that I will soon be leaving for Hawaii? By myself. While he would love to be able to pack his bags and return to the place where he proposed to me. How am I going to break the news to him?

I have an appointment in town and the bus will be here in fifteen minutes. What shall I do? Call Sander right now? I'll have to tell him I'm booking a flight, because the travel agent has given me a deal that expires tomorrow.

My mouth is so dry I can hardly swallow. "Hey there, San," I begin tentatively and inquire how he's feeling.

"I feel good! I've just had my magnesium shot and I'm about to go on a short bike ride. How are you doing, Li?"

Stay calm, I whisper to myself. I shouldn't overwhelm him with my enthusiasm. "Well, uh... I've been accepted to go and work on a farm on Hawaii!"

Silence.

"Really?"

Silence.

"That's great, Li! But what is all this?! Way to go, girl! You totally deserve it!" I get a lump in my throat; his words are so kind and encouraging.

"But how does this make *you* feel?"

And then the bus arrives.

"Isn't this your big dream? Well, then you should go and buy a ticket right away."

"You're so sweet, San," I say in a soft voice, while handing the bus driver some change for my ticket.

I feel like a traitor.

"I can't wait to read all about your adventures on our blog. I've got to go now, because they need to disconnect the IV. Love you, Li. *Aloha!*"

12 Two weeks

The first rays of sunlight burst through the clouds while I take a bite of my quark cheese with cinnamon and walnuts, followed by a large spoon of orange flavored fish oil. I hold my nose and swallow the disgusting stuff. Ever since I've started taking this "pure gold for the brain" my emotions have stopped ricocheting from intense highs to all-time lows.

That I feel calmer and better about myself also has to do with the fact that I no longer have to take care of Sander. I'm slowly regaining my strength and am now actually able to be a bigger support for him. I can now encourage him to quit drinking with the help of the well-known Dutch Jellinek Clinic. But it's going to be incredibly difficult, because the disease has gone into overdrive.

And then Sander suddenly calls me. "Li!" It sounds like he's panicking. "I'm on my way to hospital for some tests. My temperature hasn't dropped below a steady 104 since last night."

My heart rate instantly shoots up, but I manage to keep my voice relatively steady when I answer. "I'll come right over. Call me as soon as you know more. Good luck, dearie."

Walking past the intensive care, the musty smell of hospital food and chemical detergents instantly invokes old demons of fear. I take a deep breath and walk on briskly. When the fear slowly subsides I heave a deep sigh of relief.

It takes me ten minutes to get to Sander's room. He's stretched out on the bed underneath a flimsy light blue sheet that is pulled right up to his chin. At the bottom his sneakers are sticking out. Typical Sander, ready to leave the hospital as soon as he gets the green light. I am however slightly shocked by the position he is in. He's lying there as someone who's just died: eyes closed, hands folded over his chest. Thank God I can see his chest moving.

"Hi, Li," he whispers softly. "I'm really, really tired. Is it okay if you just sit here for a while, without talking?"

I lean over to kiss him softly on his lips and forehead. "Of course. I'll give you Reiki, to help you relax." As soon as I lay my warm hands on his chest, Sander immediately falls into a deep sleep. I feel an intense sadness come over me. He doesn't deserve to suffer like this. I call in all the help from above and ask them to assist him. And then, all of a sudden, I see a shadow on the white wall behind Sander's bed. I look around to see what's causing it. But there's no one there. I wonder how long Sander will hang in there. When will he die?

"Two weeks," he mutters, suddenly wide awake, spooked by his own voice. "Did I just say 'two weeks'?" He shoots me a puzzled look. "That's weird. Why did I say that?"

I can't move. Did he just answer my question? Did he answer my thoughts? I'm gasping for breath.

13 Fried fish

A new week and a drastic change of weather. In two, three days the temperature will go from a mild 68 to a scorching 95, precisely on Wednesday, which is the day I'm leaving. And today I'm going over to see Sander. "I can't really do much," he had WhatsApped me last night, just after he'd suggested going for a drive to IJmuiden Harbor to have some fried cod fish with remoulade sauce. So instead we will now probably just spend the afternoon in the back yard. When I drive off and turn the first corner it suddenly hits me that we will probably never again take the A2-freeway together on our way to friends or family. "Come on, think positive!" I reprimand myself. I want to be strong when I see Sander; for him and for me. Saying goodbye is difficult enough as it is.

When I open the glove compartment to take out the front panel of the car radio I find Sander's lucky bottle covered with little purple and pink stones, a Buddha that's no bigger than the top of my pinkie finger, and a horse shoe. All useless; we haven't had luck on our side for quite a while now.

I turn on the radio and hear Madonna sing: *There's no greater power than the power of goodbye.* Those lyrics are awfully apt. I quickly swerve the car into a lay-by and listen to the song with bated breath.

The rest of the drive goes by in slow motion. I follow the A2. I take the exit to Haarlem and IJmuiden. With an already wet sleeve I wipe away the tears. On my right I pass the blast furnaces. I turn into the street where his parents live. I park the car, I get out. It's a sweltering afternoon.

"Be strong now," I repeat to myself. A few seconds later I'm in the garden and see Sander sitting there.

"Hi, Li," Sander says in a low voice. I plant a kiss on his dry lips and forehead.

"I'm so tired. I've got to catch my breath, okay," he apologizes. "Did I startle you? Because of the way I look?"

I take in his worn-out body that's all skin and bones, slumped in the garden chair. He's dressed in jogging pants with the white/red Kangaroos sneakers we bought in Berlin last year. He's wearing a long-sleeved shirt to hide the livid scratch marks, and his fingernails are clipped to prevent further damage to his already frail, dry skin. Sander used to be such an incredibly good-looking guy; now he's thin as a rake, his cheeks are hollow, his eyes empty, and his collarbone, his elbows and his knees stick out. I can't hold back the tears any longer. His biggest fear has become reality: the disease has emaciated him. Sander straightens the back of his chair and looks at me with eyes full of love.

"Sorry, San, this is just so awful."

He takes a cigarette from the pack of Marlboro Lights on the table and lights up. "I've started smoking again. I might as well, right." He inhales deeply, followed by a terrible coughing fit. He gives me a furtive glance and cracks up. "It's happened, Li. I've become one of those pathetic cancer cases, smoking a cigarette while already lighting the next one." His remark lightens the mood and we both manage to laugh at the whole situation.

Sander takes his iPad from the oak garden table. "I'd like you to listen to this." He clicks on a video. Curious, I look at the girl behind the microphone. Wait, I know who that is. She's called Maaike Ouboter and became famous after her performance on *The Best Singer-Songwriter of the Netherlands*, a TV-program on Channel 3.

> *You kiss me, you hush me*
> *Embrace me and shush me*
> *You catch me, you crave me*
> *And infinitely unscare me*
> *You call me, you hear me*
> *You save and upset me*
> *Believe me, deprive me*
> *And smother and stun me*
>
> *You breathe and you live me*
> *You shiver and shake me*
> *You trust me*
> *You consider me a person*
>
> *And prevent me from heated dreams*
> *That rise to the surface*
> *The lonely questions*
> *of finite joy*

I know this is Sander's way of telling me something, as he so often does with lyrics; he borrows the words he can't come up with from this angel-like song.

I press on the pause button. I can't listen to this. I'd break down and then I would cancel my flight in order to stay here, to stay next to him, until it's time for him to leave this world. And neither of us has the strength to do that.

If we stay together physically, we can't let each other go, and Sander wouldn't be able to leave. He'd want to be strong for my sake and I would slowly die with him. We have to be apart to be able to let each other go. This awful but inevitable understanding has manifested itself in all crystal clarity; both in Sander and me.

It feels very ambivalent to leave Sander behind with his greatest fears, the fears I always believed I could soothe. But I now know I cannot save him, precisely because I've tried so hard to do that these past years, and in doing so I neglected my own cry for help.

"I'm really sorry, San, I'd rather listen to it some other time. It's too upsetting right now."

He nods. "Let's go for a drive then." After I've carefully helped him up, he shuffles towards the living room excruciatingly slowly and collapses in the nearest chair. "I need to rest a bit, okay? The fever really did me in. I'm dog-tired."

After another coughing fit that seems to last forever, we waddle to the car arm in arm. All the force of this once strong man - the man who could easily floor me with one arm - has been eaten away by the cancer cells. But although his muscles and fat might be gone, his willpower and sense of humor are as strong as ever.

"My booty is gone, so I now have to sit on a few pathetic little bones. And believe you me, that's not very pleasant," he says with an exaggerated local IJmuiden-accent as soon as we're both sitting in the car. "Oh yes, please watch out when you reverse, sweetheart. The street is kind of narrow."

I put my hand on his knee. "Aren't you the cutest co-driver ever," I tease him. He laughs and removes my hand from his knee. "I'd rather you didn't touch me, my skin is prickling like hell again."

With my stomach in knots we drive to the harbor. In a neighborhood with lots of speed bumps, I can almost feel his pain.

"Every bump causes weird stabs in my stomach and sternum. Just drive slowly, okay," he mutters, frustrated. "Dammit, I can't even go for a short drive with you anymore."

I'm now almost sick with worry. "Shouldn't we go back?"

He shakes his head. "No, we're not going back, we're going to have us some *kibbeling!*"

"What kind of fried fish would you like, sweetie pie?" asks the platinum blond lady with an oily brown, suntanned skin behind the counter.

"Kibbeling for two, pleazze," I answer, involuntarily mimicking her accent. I momentarily feel like a tourist in my own country. Ten minutes later we're back in the car, just in time before it starts pouring. I impatiently pull the steaming hot pieces of fish apart to make them cool down more quickly. Silently we stare at the water in front of us, with small waves sloshing against the sides of colorful fishing boats.

"Just like Saint-Tropez, huh," I break the silence, feeding Sander a piece of fish.

He rolls down the window and throws a piece to two mangy-looking doves. A snow white gull the size of a goose throws himself onto the scrumptious snack, snatches it away from the other two birds, and flies off to a wooden pole where he devours it within one second. Sander examines the scene full of interest. "I thought doves were like rats but that gull sure acts like one."

The disease is temporarily out of the picture when we drive on, past the locks, headed in the direction of the city of Beverwijk. We talk about the journey I'm about to depart on and about the week the two of us spent on Hawaii last year.

"Promise that you'll take loads of pictures and write about everything you experience on your blog? That way I can kind of travel along." About what the next weeks have in store for him, he speaks very matter-of-factly. "We'll see how it goes. I just don't know how long I can keep this up. I've been thinking about euthanasia. Not right now, but maybe in two months or so."

And then he asks me: "Would you come back then?"

I park the car by the water with a view of the locks.

"If you should decide to do that, then call me. But it could all happen very suddenly." I attempt to get through to him.

He looks away and stares at the water for a little while. "No, I'm the one who decides when it's over. So would you come or not?"

A flock of gulls rides the sea wind, floating towards Forteiland. My heart is torn apart by his question. I love him so much and of course I want to be there for him should he want me to be there. But I will be very far away.

"If you need me, I'll come back for you."

A couple of birds land on a flag pole, another group settles down in the green yellowish grass.

"But San," I continue, trying to brace myself for what I'm about to say, "I don't know if I will be there for the cremation. I'd prefer to say goodbye to you in Hawaii. By myself, surrounded by nature and in total silence. I have a feeling we are going to see each other there, just like you said when you told me about the legend of Naupaka."

Sander's attention shifts towards the fort in the middle of the Amsterdam-Rhine Canal. "Do you see that island over there? Me and the guys once went there, for a house party. It was totally crazy. They took you there with little boats."

And then he turns back to me with weary-red eyes. "I will come and visit you there together with your dad. We'll be dressed in Hawaiian shirts with big colored flowers on them and I will pinch you in your bum." He smiles and sighs deeply.

"We'll just see how it goes, Liedje. We'll keep in touch and I will call you once the end is near. Who knows, maybe I'll still be here in three months. Let's go home now, okay?"

Back home Sander immediately installs himself in the lounge chair outside and closes his eyes. He's petered-out. "We've had it good, right?" His voice sounds forceless. "All those vacations, the parties, the meals."

I kneel down next to him with tears in my eyes and give him a long, tender kiss on the lips. "A bit dry, right?" he says while exhaling, looking up at my face. "You'd better go now, Li."

We both know we should get this over with, because every second feels like a knife stab in my heart. We hug each other, we cry and we comfort each other for what will probably be, the last time ever. I kiss his forehead, taking in his scent. If only I could put it in a jar and take it with me forever and ever. I wince. My buddy, my everything. Dammit, this is *so* unfair. I want to grow old with him so badly.

"Ah, Liedje," he says, but those words only provoke a new gush of tears.

Sander is the only one who gets me, who *really* knows me. Sometimes he actually knows me better than I know myself, like when I'm feeling down and he manages to make me snap out of it, with music or with a smile. With whom will I be able to share all our memories? What will be left of me once Sander is gone? Who am I without him? We grew up together and have shaped each other into the persons we are now.

What is he thinking right now? Does he also feel this is our final goodbye? Yes, because otherwise he wouldn't have said that we had it so good. He must be feeling terribly sad, but I don't dare ask him. It would make our goodbye even more painful, and besides, I already know the answer.

I muster up all my courage and start walking to the kitchen

door, with feet that feel like they're made of lead. "Wait, I've completely forgotten to wish you a good trip!" Sander calls after me cheerfully. I look back once more and see how his life energy has slowly seeped away. This past hour he's pretended to feel better and stronger than he actually feels. It confirms my decision that I should go to Hawaii. We have to let each other go in order to spare each other even more agony and suffering.

But what an incredibly difficult life lesson this is.

"And don't forget to enjoy yourself. Will you do that, on behalf of both of us? *Lobi,* I love you, sweetie."

PART 3
REDISCOVERY
HAWAII, SUMMER 2013
THE BEGINNING OF A
HEALING JOURNEY

14   The Flight

What am I doing?! How in the world am I going to do this, 24 hours in an airplane, all by myself? The walls are already closing in on me now. My heart is pounding. I'm scared and feel an overpowering urge to make a run for it. What have I done? I can't just leave and leave Sander behind with all his fears and pain. He feels safe and comfortable with me. What if he dies in two weeks and I won't be there? He needs me!

I can vividly picture his hollow eyes and his lower arms full of red scratch marks and think of the itching that drives him crazy; like a million pinpricks, that's how he described it. He spent hours lying next to me on the couch, cherishing my soft touch on his painful skin. That was the only way he was able to fall into a deep sleep. Although I was glad to be able to do that for him, I desperately longed for his hands on my skin as well.

My throat feels so tight I don't manage to swallow my food and I feel nauseous just thinking about the fact that the distance between Sander and me is growing by the minute: 7306 miles to be exact. My heart rate and respiration instantly skyrocket again. *Don't go and hyperventilate now.* I try to pull myself together.

Maybe I should distract myself with a movie or leaf through a magazine? I pull the hefty cream-colored Diesel bag from underneath the seat in front of me, put it on my lap and rummage through it like a drug addict craving a shot. *Lip gloss, keys and homemade almond flour cupcakes.* I can see the man sitting next to me is keeping an eye on me. Does he realize I'm on the verge of a nervous breakdown?

Ah! Found it. I take out a canvas tote bag with the words "white light" written on it in big letters. Juuls sent me this in the mail. On the covering note she'd written: "This bag will protect you wherever you go."

Slightly disappointed I look at the first magazine I dig up: my mom's *Libelle,* a sort of *Good Housekeeping.*

As soon as I turn to the first page I notice the envelope I had stuck there right before I left. It's a card from Ester, one of my oldest girlfriends. I stare out the airplane window at the fluffy cloud cover. Should I read it? I bet she's written terribly sweet, comforting words that will really get to me, but I nevertheless decide to tear open the green envelope. Inside is a glossy card with a picture of fall foliage and white rays of light; the inside is filled with her tiny blue handwriting.

> *Dear Lide,*
>
> *For Christmas you sent me an angel card with the words "have faith." After the difficult birth of our first baby, Ilija, it was not self-evident that we would be able to have another healthy child. A week before I delivered I wasn't sure anymore if I'd made the right choice. Was inducing labor for our second son indeed the best thing to do?*
>
> *I took your angel card with me to hospital and right before I went into labor I repeated that to myself: "Have faith." When they administered the first dose of medicine I instantly felt very calm. I had faith and could let go of my fears. A few hours later I was crying tears of happiness over the birth of our healthy son Daniel.*
>
> *This is all a fairly long introduction for what I want to wish you. Dear Lide, have faith in yourself and trust you've made the right choice to embark on this beautiful journey.*

Have faith in the people you hold dear in Holland. They support your decision. Have faith and try to let go of your fears. And don't forget to enjoy all the wonderful adventures you will experience.

She signs off with a small drawing of a guardian angel. I hide my face behind my gray linen shawl so that no one can see I'm crying. Her words instantly make all my fears and the thousands of doubts - big and small ones - vanish into thin air.

Ester is right. I have to let go of my fears and stick to my decision. This journey is meant as a way to heal myself, not to run away from all the agony.

On Big Island I want to let go of the connections and all the conditioning from the past. The 33-year old exhausted journalist from Holland is going to be put on ice and the young woman I also happen to be is going to get cracking! I'm going to work up a nice sweat in the tropical heat of the jungle. I'm going to do things, learn things! Maybe within three months I will know what my mission in life is and what really drives me. Or maybe I won't. *"Anyway the wind blows."* I'll see how things turn out. That thought relaxes me and helps me nod off to sleep.

"We expect to reach our final destination of Los Angeles within an hour." When the pilot's voice breaks the silence in the airplane cabin, I wake with a start. *Where am I?* Oh yeah, in a Boeing 737 somewhere over the United States. My legs feel numb because I've been lying in a crooked position. It's dark in the plane and most passengers are still snoozing just like I was. My oversized neighbor is making soft snoring noises. Luckily I have an aisle seat so that I can go to the lavatories without having to disturb anyone. I walk towards the back of the plane where the stewardesses are chatting in low voices. Their powdered faces and bright red lips light up in the sunlight. *How do they manage to look so impeccable after a ten hour's flight?!*

I walk to one of the windows, wondering where we are. Below I see a dry, yellowish brown expanse and a river that cuts a jagged line through the landscape. Wait a minute, I recognize this! We're flying over Arizona. That's the Colorado River, flowing towards Lake Powell, where the Hoover Dam provides Greater Las Vegas with power. This is unbelievable! Exactly ten months ago Sander and I drove there, in a big gray Jeep, with our best selection of house and pop music blaring out the speakers.

Maybe in a few weeks he will be taking this same route, flying over all our beautiful memories in Arizona, Death Valley and Utah...

I cover my face with my shawl again. Luckily someone comes out of the lavatory at that moment so that I can break down without any onlookers. The acute sadness has returned in full force. I wish I could kick and scream and vent my emotions, but instead I yell out in silence. "Why can't Sander and I be together?" I look at my reflection in the mirror and try to wipe away the black mascara streaks with a handkerchief. *God, I miss you so, San.*

And then something peculiar happens. I have to try to calm the thoughts racing through my head in order to be able to make out the words I hear: "You will see each other again in Hawaii."

Could that be my guardian angel's voice, right here in this smelly cubicle of an airplane lavatory?

"Please return to your seats," the captain announces over the intercom. *Well, that leaves little to the imagination.* I try to laugh away the tension and stroll back to my seat, preparing for landing and the transfer for the last leg of the journey to Big Island.

15   Aloha, Big Island!

My heart skips a beat. On the horizon of the endless blue expanse of the Pacific Ocean below us I catch my first glimpse of the mountain tops of Oahu, the most famous of the Hawaiian islands. I still can't believe that I'm going to live here for a while, on one of most secluded archipelago's in the whole world.

Only a year ago I considered Hawaii as a pilgrimage destination for surf fanatics and a vacation paradise for wealthy Americans who want to tie the knot on one of its many sandy white beaches. I also know President Barack Obama was born and raised on Oahu, that the box office hit *Jurassic Park* was filmed near the jagged cliffs of Kaua'i, and that on December 7th, 1941 a large part of the US naval fleet was destroyed in Pearl Harbor. But the island group is so much more than a commercialized colony and an important moment in world history according to the magazine on my lap. "Together with New Zealand and Easter Island, Hawaii makes up the so-called Polynesian Triangle. The native inhabitants live in harmony with nature. Old traditions, rituals and legends are closely intertwined with the modern way of life. The original population of Big Island makes offerings of red flowers, wine and chocolate to Pele, the Goddess of Fire," the article continues, "hoping to pacify her explosive power with which she obliterated the village of Kalapana in 1990." The article even mentions the legend of Naupaka, with an illustration of the half-flowers. The caption reads: "Hawaiians believe that naupaka flowers will one day grow back towards each other and that the two lovers will eventually be reunited."

Did Sander perhaps read this magazine article before he proposed to me?

It would appear the Fire Goddess has ruthlessly driven a wedge between the two of us as well, although I'd rather believe Sander's revised version, that says we have to let each other go so that we will one day become one again. Shall we really see each other again at the foot of Pele's volcano on Big Island, like that voice out of nowhere told me just now?

As soon as the stewardess opens the door of the airplane, the humid air falls over me like a warm blanket. I instantly recognize the refreshingly sweet scent of the Hawaiian frangipani flowers. On my way through the arrivals hall towards the luggage belt, flanked by banana trees and hibiscus flowers, I suddenly realize how recently we walked here as a newly engaged couple. I went to the restrooms at one point and Sander decided to surprise me with a lei, a Hawaiian flower necklace, which I wore until the very last flower wilted.

I take a taxi to a cheap little hotel near the famous Waikiki Beach, where I will spend one night before flying on to Big Island. "Bummer!" I cry out as soon as I see my room. There is barely enough space for a double bed and the window is almost completely obscured by the air conditioning unit. "Penny wise, pound foolish," I admonish myself. However, when I discover that the Wi-Fi connection works and I read all the messages from home, I immediately lighten up.

While half of Holland is stuck in traffic on their way to work, I go out to the narrow concrete balcony and stand there looking up at the stars. I sit down on one of the white plastic chairs and mull over the next couple of months.

Is this the start of a new beginning? When I eventually return home my life won't be the same as it was. I close my eyes and listen to the siren of a police car; it reminds me of the piercing New York version. Sander and I stayed in the Trump SoHo Hotel for a week and we saw countless many police cars rush by the floor-to-ceiling windows. Sander, who had just been through another session of very heavy chemo, got an incredible amount of energy from the city. It was the best week of our lives. We ate Texan chicken wings in an all-night restaurant, with crisp linen table cloths and waiters dressed in white aprons and cargo shorts. We took a helicopter ride over the Manhattan skyline, Brooklyn and the Yankee Stadium in the Bronx; a present from my eldest brother and sister-in-law, who wanted to give us an unforgettable experience to try to help us momentarily forget our awful plight. Sander would be undergoing an allogeneic stem cell transplant a few weeks after our vacation, with a real possibility he would not survive. We lived like kings in a doomed empire, where the foundation was already showing subtle cracks.

That night I dream of a fawn that urges me to follow her. We run through white sterile hallways that remind me of the University Hospital in Utrecht. The little animal slows down in front of a door but walks right into the room without so much as a pause. I tentatively peer into the large space. I see Sander, stretched out on a transparent bed of crystal, or at least that's what it looks like. He's very happy to see me and straightens up. "I'm coming with you," he cries out eagerly, but something prevents him from getting up. And then we both see that his real body is still lying on the bed but that he is no longer in it.

I wake up, bathing in sweat, and quickly reach for the light switch.

As soon as my eyes have adjusted to the light and I make

out the contours of the closet and that awful air conditioning unit, I realize where I am. I am alone in a hotel in Honolulu. When I remember my dream I feel sick to my stomach. I really need to go outside, I need to get out of this cramped space, away from the thoughts in my head and jogging is the best remedy I can think of. I put on my running gear and walk out of the hotel, where birds are already announcing the new morning with their song.

I start running over the boulevard, where the first surfers are wading into the dark sea. Half an hour later the first rays of sun light up Oahu's coastline. This definitely is a sweet smelling paradise full of flowers! Normally this would blow my mind but now I'm just running like a mad woman, trying to outrun my depression. I dash up a steep hill as if it's nothing. When I reach the top I take a break to marvel at the mighty ocean at my feet. On a bench at the edge of a cliff two turtle doves are doing the same thing. I am gripped by a wave of nostalgia. I wince; I'm feeling so incredibly sad and homesick.

"Is there anyone up there who can help me?" I stretch out my arms in a helpless gesture. This whole Hawaii thing is going to be a disaster. If I am going to feel this torn up inside, I might as well go back. And just when I want to head back to the hotel, at my wit's end, I see a splendid rainbow that stretches from the ocean to the mountain side. This natural wonder manages to make me snap out of it and I head back down to Waikiki Beach feeling elated. On the way I notice a large boulder with a drawing of an eye with angel wings on it. The message is loud and clear: the angels are keeping watch over me. I should seek solace in small miracles like these.

The last stretch of my journey to Big Island has commenced. My new home is only a thirty minutes flight from Honolulu, but the airline announces a delay of no less than three hours.

I quickly find out I should never have booked with the budget airline company "Go!"; there's a long line of complainers in front of the desk. "It's always the same old song with you people," says a guy with a full head of brown curls. He turns towards his girlfriend, a small blond girl with a suntanned, athletic body that almost makes me green with envy. "It's about time they scrap the exclamation mark in their name." Me and a few other passengers chuckle at his joke.

When we finally board the small propeller plane three hours later, with the word GO! painted on it in giant letters, I get the giggles because I imagine climbing onto the wing with a can of black spray paint and changing the exclamation mark to a question mark.

Thirty minutes later we touch down on Big Island and again all sorts of things go wrong. Lewis, the manager of the Hawaiian Sanctuary, isn't there. My text with my new arrival time has apparently not reached him. When I try to call him, it turns out I have the wrong number.

An old man with long, gray-white hair and a beard rushes to my aid. He discovers that the number I have is missing a digit and after another try a sleepy-sounding Lewis answers the phone. "I'll be there in forty-five minutes," he says to my relief. I walk to the luggage belt for my backpack, only to discover it's completely empty. Could someone have stolen it? *Of course not, no need to panic,* I try to reassure myself while walking through the deserted arrivals hall with my nerves on tenterhooks. Where is everybody? *"Aloha?"* I call out with a touch of despair in my voice. Somewhere a door opens. "Aloha!" I call out again, but this time a bit louder. A small Hawaiian girl waves me over and hands me my backpack from behind the counter. *"Mahalo,"* I thank her in Hawaiian, haul my luggage outside and sit down on a bench with a good view of the parking lot. Above me the speakers are playing soft Hawaiian welcoming music. When I strain my ears I make out a ukulele and the voice of my favorite Hawaiian singer Israel Kamakawiwo'ole!

I recognize "Somewhere over the Rainbow", a song Sander and I used to sing along to in our Ford Mustang C convertible on Kaua'i. I wonder how Sander is doing and reread the last message I sent him, in which I wrote that I think of him often and am sending him love. My heart feels heavy when I reread his reply.

JUNE 21, 2013

Sander:
"I'm at home and having trouble with oxygen, an iron deficiency; everything. I'm not going to embellish it: I've hit my tailbone very, very hard when I fell. I dream about Hawaii a lot. Go for it! xx"

Typical Sander. Despite all the shit he continues to support me. I know communicating is difficult for him and I really want to support him although I also need him badly right now.

Li:
"You're strong, sweet and beautiful and I wish you were here. I dreamt that you'd left your body behind and wanted to come with me. Meanwhile I'm sitting here, waiting at the airport. Love you. It goes deep. This is so hard. Kiss, sweetie."

Sander:
"Hang in there. This is your last station! Xx."

That really helps; it gives me strength. I'm ready for my new home.

16   Clear thoughts

A black SUV stops in front of the bench I'm sitting on and out climbs a muscular man who looks kind of Asian. He could be Korean. Wait a minute... Lewis, Korean?! Not quite what I'd expected. But he must be here for me because there's still not a soul in sight at the airport. The man, who I guess must be in his early thirties, walks up to me. "Aloha." He gives me a hug, picks up my black Nomad backpack and effortlessly throws it into the back of his Nissan pick-up truck. A man of few words but all the more deeds, I conclude.

As soon as I get in next to him, I immediately feel much calmer. After two days of traveling I've finally reached Big Island; I'm now near Fire Goddess Pele. When Lewis asks me why I'm late, I only say: "Go! Airlines." He smiles understandingly.

Lewis tells me he worked as a marine in the US Army for several years and wanted to make a fresh start after military service and thus decided to leave his hometown Detroit. He'd set his mind on Alaska, but then met someone who told him about the Hawaiian Sanctuary. He adjusted his plans and ever since has been the manager of the self-sustaining farm on the property. "I moved from a mild to a tropical climate," he tells me in a thick American accent. "It took me a while to get used to the humid jungle. It rains practically every day but you'll soon find out for yourself what that means."

We leave the paved road and turn into a track made of

black earth with big rocks and deep potholes from all the rain. "Welcome to the Hawaiian Sanctuary," says Lewis, gesturing straight ahead. In the headlights of the car I make out a long lane flanked by banana trees and tropical flowers. I recognize the orange parrot's beak I used to buy on the flower market in Utrecht; Sander's favorite. He would arrange them in empty apple juice bottles, in a perfect cluster, just like a stylist for *Home and Garden* would do.

And then I notice I'm being watched: on the other side of my car window a pair of eager caramel-colored eyes look up at me. A dog! How nice! The thin little animal with shiny black fur is running in front of the car quite precariously. "Kalani," Lewis warns him through his open window. A tall man appears on the path to shoo the dog away. "She's afraid of chickens but loves to chase car tires. Crazy animal..." says Lewis.

We drive past a building with a green roof on big green poles. "That's the lounge area, the hangout for the people that live here. At the back of that building is the wellness center with a sauna and a Jacuzzi. You're welcome to use it on Tuesdays, Thursdays and during the weekend."

It sounds too good to be true. I sure am going to make use of that.

"You'll be sharing a room with two Japanese girls in one of our *jungalows*. I'll take you there right away. A *jungalow?* That probably means a bungalow in the jungle. We drive on over a narrow track with loads of big ferns and long orchids with white flowers and purple hearts that brush against the side of the car. Kalani is still running in front of us although her barking is drowned out by an orchestra of strange, computer-like sounds.

"Oh, that's the coquí frogs; they were brought here from Puerto Rico in the eighties," Lewis explains. "The islanders consider them a pest, and not only because of the sound - you get used to that - but mainly because of the damage they inflict on the indigenous flora and fauna. They devour absolutely everything!"

Hmm, thank God I've brought ear plugs.

In front of us I see a pretty basic, square cabin-like structure, with wall dividers made of sturdy gauze. Lewis parks the car and deposits my backpack in front of the swinging door.

"If you feel like it, you're more than welcome to come and meet the others. We'll be in the lounge."

I thank him for the ride and dump my backpack on the floor in my new accommodation. Two basic lamps light up a space of about 160 square feet, with three wooden beds and plastic dressers in it. The back bed on the left has no sheets on it. That'll be mine then. I listen intently to the frog sounds coming from the jungle behind the little house; there must be thousands of them. "Cookie?" I distinctly hear them call their own name. A bird disturbs their monotonous noise with another funny call. "Waikiki?" I burst out laughing. This is crazy. It's like the animals are communicating with me, because I have in fact just come from Waikiki Beach and would not half mind a cookie. I send Sander a text:

21 JUNE 2013

Li:
"I've arrived! What an unbelievable place! There are weird croaking frogs everywhere. I'll be sleeping in a sort of tent with two Japanese roommates. I can hear the rain on the canvas. Kiss."

I'm surprised to see that Sander replies with the previous text he sent me.

Quickly followed by another one.

Oh God, he's deteriorating rapidly. I've got to find some kind of distraction, otherwise I won't be able to resist the urge to return to Holland. Ten minutes later I switch on my flashlight and carefully pick my way through the wet grass towards the lounge area.

With the pitch dark forest all around me it's almost like the sky is closing down on me. The Milky Way is like a white airbrush line, surrounded by millions of twinkling stars. I stand there for a while, breathlessly staring up at the sky. Because of the alien-like amphibian noises and these vivid celestial bodies, Big Island kind of feels like a different planet altogether. I decide then and there I'm not going to tell anyone here what's happening at home, so that I won't have to be confronted by it all the time.

"The spot where you sleep is a vortex, a power spot," Bob explains to me a few minutes later. Bob is the financial advisor of the Hawaiian Sanctuary and lives here. "Many people experience a deep sense of calm and sleep like a baby." He's leaning against a sort of massage table, where my two Japanese roommates, Akiko and Maya, are busy with an iMac and iPad. Bob is tall, looks like he's in his early fifties, has blond curly hair, a short beard with wisps of gray, and sparkling bright blue eyes.

"And this bed right here is filled with crystals, to help your body relax," he continues, in high spirits. "You can adjust the temperature; that's what the Japanese girls do."

Akiko, with a full head of midnight black hair and a square jaw line, joins in: "It's good to warm up your muscles before you go to sleep, 'cause the nights can be pretty dank." Maya looks at Akiko with question marks in her eyes. Akiko quickly repeats Bob's story for her in terse, short Japanese sentences. Maya nods in agreement. With her white powdered face, bright red lipstick and a thick black line under her eyes she's a classic Japanese beauty; she would make the perfect geisha.

"Aloha, gals," says Bob, giving each of us a bear hug, "I'm off to bed." I'm still not quite used to this enthusiastic physical greeting, although it does beat the traditional three kisses with which Dutch people greet each other, a custom everyone secretly hates but no one dares to admit that.

"Can I ask you something?" I quickly say, before he's gone. "Can you actually feel Pele's energy here?" I explain that I've read a lot about her power but decide not to mention the legend of Naupaka.

"Oh yeah!" Bob replies with a mysterious smile on his lips. Akiko closes her laptop and listens intently. "It's a pretty potent energy too, not everyone can handle it," Bob continues. Some people don't even manage to stay here a whole week. People can become extremely depressed or explosively hyperactive."

He explains that the mood you were in when you arrived on the island is reinforced. "Think of it as a volcano eruption. All the overheated emotional weight is thrust out." His tone becomes more serious: "Make sure you keep your thoughts positive, because everything you think about could come true, including the negative thoughts." Again a mischievous smile appears on his lips. "Don't forget that, ladies. Think positive!

You'll find out soon enough what I mean."

Thirty minutes later I'm in bed but I can't get Bob's words out of my head. Staying positive 100 percent of the time is kind of difficult with everything that's going on in my life right now. If Sander dies, I will feel heartbroken. What if I collapse when my emotions erupt?

And then I remember Elijah, the angel of Hanalei Bay, who taught me the deeper meaning of surfing: "The waves symbolize the flow of life. And you can only ride them if you let go of all your thoughts, and trust where nature is taking you."

17 Pele calls me to her

"Waikiki." A bright red bird wakes me with its remarkable call. It's perched on a leaf in one of the banana trees behind Akiko's bed. The gauze barrier between us and the tropical outside is not exactly soundproof. The bird whizzes off the moment a loud booming sound disturbs its song. Three loud booming sounds! *What is that?* Akiko and Maya wake up. Akiko regards me with sleepy eyes and swings one of her legs off the mattress. "Did you sleep well?" she asks, and then, seeing the surprise on my face: "Oh, that's the cook, he blows on a conch shell to let us know breakfast is served. In fifteen minutes he will do it again and we all have to be in the kitchen by then.

Maya is obviously not a morning person. Sighing, she rolls over on her back and mutters something in Japanese; probably some kind of complaint about having to get up so early. I quickly put on a pair of Adidas shorts, a T-shirt and my silver-gray Havaiana's, or rather my Hawaiana's - the same ones I re-baptized in Kaua'i when we were there ten months ago.

On the way to the kitchen I hardly know where to look. On the pictures on the website this place already looked like paradise, but the real-life version is even better and more beautiful, with scented flowers in beautiful colors absolutely everywhere. On the ground I see small, yellow clovers as well as cup-shaped red ones with long, sturdy stems. I see huge bunches of miniature bananas hanging under bright green, long leaves. Closer to the ground, in between pointy silver green spikes, I spot pineapples. Further on I recognize the green yellowish fruit of the papaya at the top of 10-feet high trunks. And then the cook blows his conch shell again and at 8 o'clock sharp everyone is indeed in the kitchen.

Just like in our jungalow, the area is walled off with thick green gauze. Next to the sink I see a narrow tropical wooden counter with all sorts of goodies on it. But not warm croissants or rolls with cold cuts and jam, because carbohydrates and sugar are unhealthy according to the philosophy of the Hawaiian Sanctuary. No, instead I see eggs, fresh pineapple and a rich chocolate smoothie sweetened with bananas and honey. Everything is grown right here on the property. "Even the raw cacao," the cook proudly tells me. He looks to be about my age, is dressed in harem pants and a turban, and has a long beard. If you'd failed to notice the clear blue eyes and American accent, you'd think he was from the Middle-East. He introduces himself as J., hugs me and then regards me very intently for a moment or two. I stand there shifting from one leg to the other and feel the heat rising up my neck. Luckily he turns his attention back to the smoothie and starts explaining: "Raw cacao is the most antioxidant-rich food in the world. It contains up to seven times more antioxidants than processed cocoa and more than red wine, açai berries or blueberries. In short, it's superfood!"

That is music to my ears; if I want to live a healthy life it means I will have to drink as much of this heavenly concoction as possible. *Hmm, I can think of worse things.* It gets even better when J. tells me that the Mayans and Aztecs used raw cacao to enhance their inner journey. The compounds in the dark matter, adrenaline and theobromine, increase the blood flow to the brain and make your blood vessels dilate, causing the skin to absorb more oxygen. The effect of that is not only an incredible amount of energy, but also feelings of euphoria.

"It makes it easier to let go of emotional burdens and feel love for everything and everyone," the cook adds.

In other words, healthy ecstasy, I conclude. I fill a mug to the brim and join Akiko and Maya. I wish I could do this for hours, sipping my smoothie while enjoying the view of the grounds with the chickens quietly foraging underneath the tropical flowers. Not needing to do anything, not having to do anything, not being anything. Muffled beats bring me back to the table. "Did you sleep well?" Lewis asks me, turning down the music on his iPhone.

"I slept absolutely wonderful!" I reply, wondering again how old this guy actually is. His tight shirt, cargo shorts and boots obscure a well-trained body and he hardly has any wrinkles on his face.

"I'm planning a hike to the spot where the lava flows into the ocean tonight. Anyone want to join me?" All heads at the table nod. "Good. We will leave at 2 a.m. sharp. That way we will be there in time for sunrise."

Unbelievable! I haven't even been on the island for 24 hours and I am already going to meet Pele!

"Lide," Lewis continues, "you don't have to start work right away. You'd better rest a bit after your long journey."

Thirty minutes later I am stretched out in a magical hammock filled with crystals, followed by a session in the sauna and the Jacuzzi. Both with an amazing view of the unspoiled jungle. Outside I see a climber full of green-orange fruit, entwined around a silver-gray tree. That's passion fruit; I recognize it from our previous trip to Hawaii. Sander and I picked them on the northern coast of Oahu, where we'd stayed in a tiny wooden lodge on the ocean front.

I decide I want to bring Pele an offering of cacao beans tonight and state an intention like the Hawaiians do. I know Sander's not well, because he isn't replying to my messages. I will ask the Goddess of Fire to help him and bring him to Big Island when it's time.

Back in the jungalow I write my intentions on a piece of paper and put it in my bag. I also ask for her help in regaining my strength. Luckily I don't find it at all difficult to catch a couple of hours of sleep before we head to the lava plain. Apparently there's more fatigue in my body than I thought.

When the alarm clock goes at 1.45 a.m. I'm instantly wide awake and quickly pull on a warm legging and a rain coat. Lewis advised us to wear adequate protective clothing because the lava rocks can be sharp. As the hike will take six hours, a bottle of water is also a must.

Akiko and Maya have a head lamp and look like tiny mine workers. At two o'clock on the dot we climb into the back of Lewis' truck so that we can look at the stars during the drive. Lewis looks like a professional hiker with his sturdy shoes, long wooden stick and compact backpack. He's also brought walking sticks along for us. "Carefully place the stick in front of you and tap on the ground, because coagulated lava can be so thin you can fall right through." He continues, in a slightly more admonishing tone: "And look out for sharp rocks and let me know the minute you scratch yourself. Even if it's just a tiny little thing. In this tropical climate a small wound can easily lead to blood infection." Lewis tells us about the cook who hurt her foot and had to be rushed off to hospital in critical condition a short while ago. "We've got a full moon to light our way," he says, pointing towards the sky. I have never before seen the dark craters this clearly with the naked eye.

"It's a supermoon," Akiko says, "this month the distance between the moon and the earth is the smallest it can be. And you can really feel that, because I haven't slept a wink." She laughs.

I observe the moon and the millions of twinkling stars from

the back of the truck. Akiko and Maya also sit there quietly staring up at the majestic sphere.

When we drive downhill the wind and soft rain buffet our faces. I estimate we've been driving downhill in one straight line for ten minutes and the closer we get to the ocean, the warmer it becomes. The rain has stopped and the rainforest is replaced by palm trees. I can easily make out their contours in the moonlight, with the shadow of their tufts that makes an elegant silhouette against the backdrop of the vast lava plain that stretches out in front of us for miles and miles. The black fields look magical, with the top lit up silver-gray in the moonlight. It is in this area, on the southeastern coast of Big Island, that Pele swallowed up an entire village with her greedy lava tongues in the early nineties. Because the eruptions of the two volcanoes, Kilauea and Mauna Loa, are usually not that violent, the inhabitants of the areas at risk could luckily pack their things in time.

Legend has it that Pele lives in the former of the two, some-where in the Halema'uma'u Crater. Lewis hasn't encountered or felt the Fire Goddess in the four years he's been living on the island, but he knows plenty of stories of people who did. As soon as we set foot on the moonlike landscape he starts to talk. "In old Hawaiian songs Pele is sometimes referred to as She-Who-Shapes-the-Sacred-Land. She can take on several different shapes. There's a story about someone who gave an old woman who was dressed completely in white a lift. She was standing on one of the roads near the Kilauea Volcano and had a small dog with her. When the driver later looked in the rear view mirror, she was gone. Apparently her face also regularly appears on photographs. I now have goose bumps over my entire body. Normally I love hearing these kind of stories, but while walking on the once burning lava streams it suddenly feels kind of spooky.

Lewis goes on: "The inhabitants of this area always speak of the ancient goddess with great respect. Not out of fear she will destroy their land, but rather because of the new land she creates. The lava streams from the Crater of Kilauea have been flowing into the ocean since 1983 and have added a little over a mile of land to the coastline."

We walk for hours and hours, clambering up and down lava-sculptures. Some look serene and smooth, others are hideously sharp and pointy, with wafer-thin edges that make squeaky sounds under the soles of our shoes – they remind me of the razor shells on Dutch beaches.

Maya's frail body is exhausted and we're forced to lower our tempo. Instead of two hours it nearly takes us four to get to the shoreline. Not that I care. For me the walk is one long meditation; I slog along behind the group without thinking. Sander's absence is so poignant it feels like a knife cutting through my soul and every time I silently weep a soft rain starts to fall. My salty tears mingle with the misty rain; as if the spirits of the island share my grief.

The Earth is carrying me. The wind tenderly dries my tears. And the moonlight eases the weight. For a while my body becomes one with the elements and the cosmos with its countless many bright stars. The magical feeling is enhanced when I spot red smoke in the distance. That's where the lava is flowing into the ocean! We're almost there! Because the lava flows in the depths beneath our feet, it's also getting hotter. We're not only on a terrain where the red-hot, churning rock reigns, but where the air we breathe could become toxic. As soon as we smell rotten eggs we have to get out of here, because that's a sure sign of the deadly sulfur dioxide gas. A few gulps of that and it's all over.

And then we're there, on one of the few spots on the planet

where new earth is actually being created. Awe-struck we look at the bright red, treacle-like mass coming out of the inclined rock, which drops into the ocean with a loud hissing sound. Enormous amounts of steam rise up where the lava - with a temperature of 212 degrees - hits the cold water. In front of the steep cliffs and the impressive spectacle of water and fire, there's a tourist boat. I wonder if it's rigged out with special armor. It must be, because otherwise the boat would disappear into the water like a knob of butter in a hot frying pan. When we walk on towards the lava stream I feel a sweltering heat underneath my shoes. I halt and look through the thin cracks in the rocks and see the bright orange lava far below.

"Wow! This is amazing!" I cry out in a rush of adrenaline.

This is the place I want to give my offering. This is the right spot. I reach into my pocket for the piece of paper and quickly slide it into the crack. It lands on the swirling mass and instantly ignites. I'm overtaken by a wave of sadness. I let go of my last bit of hope that Sander will recover and ask Pele to sever the connection between Sander and me with her fire, and to facilitate his passage to the other side.

"Pele! Help him, please help Sander and help me, reinforce me," I shout towards the smoking flank of the volcano. In one sweeping motion I scatter the cacao beans in the furnace and thank her in her own language, taking a bow with my hands clasped in front of my body. *"Mahalo nui loa!"* Having said that I walk back to the safe part of the terrain, making sure to tap the ground in front of me with my stick.

Akiko is kneeled down near the edge of the black cliffs, taking photographs of the stunning phenomenon. She doesn't notice that behind her another peculiar spectacle is taking place, where the bright red top part of the sun appears above the wide expanse of water, accompanied by orange and salmon pink hues. While to the right fire is plunging into the ocean, to the left it is rising up out of the water in the form of a sphere.

Everything is one.
Sander and I are one as well.

Forever.

18   Smile *on*

My heart is being torn apart
craving for love.
It's no longer able to beat for my love
without also taking care of itself.
So fragile and dependent on others.
So lonely in my soul,
Going back to self-love.

Halia

Total panic. Sander's condition is deteriorating rapidly and his best friend Jorn warns me via Skype that the end is near. Furious, he sobs: "Dammit, my best friend is dying right there in a bed in the living room. No more future, no more dreams. It is so fucking unfair. You two should have grown old together and had kids."

My chin is trembling when I ask if they're still able to communicate. He shakes his head. "Hardly. We've been selecting the music for his funeral, but the only thing he can do is nod when he likes something. He spaces out all the time, but then suddenly he'll be all lucid again. He's no longer the Sander I know. His temperature is 107 and he lives in a delusional world. Yesterday he insisted he had to go to Amsterdam with me. To calm him, we carried him to a chair, but of course he didn't even have the energy for that; he was exhausted."

I can vividly picture it in my mind: Sander, all determined

and grouchy, adamant to get Jorn to do what he wants. "He's still an old tiger," Jorn continues, "fighting to the death."

Jorn is right. Sander's fighting spirit is unparalleled. He eagerly grabs onto any possibility to overcome the disease. Even experimental treatments like sgn-35 that damaged his nerves. He never ever complained about the numb feet which made it difficult to walk. The opposite rather; he managed to transform his anger and helplessness into words of wisdom on Twitter, his own sounding-board. That's where he became a pillar of strength for other cancer patients like him. He even managed to help a young woman who'd given up regain her fighting mentality via an e-mail he sent her. Sander asked me to read it before sending it. I will never forget his honest and encouraging words.

Hi!

Death. It's a terrible thing to fear. I'm dealing with it, but I don't accept it. Which by the way doesn't mean I'm constantly "fighting" it. I'm actually fighting less because of it. And just that word itself already. "Fighting"... Completely overrated if you ask me. ;-)

My goal has always been to not let the illness play too big a part in my life. I've got cancer, but the cancer doesn't have me.

Most people don't understand what we're going through, others don't want to know. I too was always concerned about that. You feel good and strong and you want your environment to confirm that, to give that back to you. You want to show them that you're well, in spite of everything. That you are strong and doing a little better than before. And that despite that whole cancer thing, you are holding your ground. What I absolutely did not want, was to be PITIED. And then when people look at you like that, shit man, then suddenly you are a sorry case! Sometimes it works like a mirror: perhaps those people are right? Are you in fact more ill than you think? Maybe you're in denial? Well, no. At least I don't think so. It's just a fundamentally different way of looking at it. We've got a totally different mindset. We are glad with every step, with every bit of progress we make. Being ill also means you have to manage your environment to deal with it. ;-) Half of the time you're actually comforting the people talking to you. You have to manage them, you have to help them to start thinking the way you're thinking. How to talk to you and how to treat you in a certain way. Fuckin' bizarre!

As for counseling, for me Twitter has proved to be a real boon. It started out as a channel to vent, as I did not want to start writing one of those pathetic cancer blogs. But it soon became an information channel for the outside world. Family, friends, strangers: everyone could read it. So incredibly easy! And let me tell you, after four years I've finally kind of got it under control. And that feels so much better than the constant disappointment and anger. ;-)

Talk to you soon. Keep your back straight and smile *on*!

Even now Sander still keeps his 334 followers on Twitter informed about his illness and death process. It's often almost embarrassingly straightforward, like this message, a few days ago: "Fighting, almost dead... But not just yet!!!"

He received a lot of heartwarming reactions. "Hang in there, buddy" and: "I am sending you the most beautiful thoughts and heaps of energy."

But lately it's been awfully quiet on the social media-front.

Everyone is waiting for that one "liberating" message.

I look at Jorn's pale, skinny face. He's telling me Sander no longer eats, but does still take fluids. "Vodka," he adds with a mischievous twist around his lips. "We drink one glass every day, and a cigarette to go with it."

Despite my tears I have to laugh. "Way to go, San," I quietly sob. Jorn goes on: "The other day he called me. God, he really scared me there – because everyone thought he was in a coma – and shouted at me through the telephone: "Hey, you bastard! Where are you? I've got vodka and cigarettes here." I rushed over there so fast. We had a drink but we didn't really talk, as he was only lucid at times. But we laughed so hard when he woke and called me again, and only then realized that I was sitting next to him."

Jon tells me about the walks they made these past months. And then he says: "Sander feels terrible about hurting you with his drinking. He wants you to be able to start over, he wants that more than anything. He really believes you deserve that and still loves you like crazy." Jorn pauses for a second. "He relied too heavily on you. We discussed that as well." He shows me his fist. "Here, this is you." He clenches his other hand into a fist. "And this is Sander." He presses the last fist into the first one forcefully. "He crushed you. The pressure on your foundation became so heavy that it shattered into a million pieces. If he'd divided the weight over several people, maybe it would have been less of a burden for you. Sander was shocked when I told him this. He said he had never looked at it that way. It was really painful for him to hear."

Jorn's words really get to me. They also change the way I look at the whole thing. *Of course* I was the one who took care of Sander, *of course* I was the one who took it upon my shoulders. We always supported each other and when one of us couldn't take it anymore, the other one would always be there. That balance is what made our relationship so strong. Until the point when neither of us had the energy to support the other anymore. That's when our safety net fell through.

"Thank you for helping us realize that," I sob. "And thank you for being there for Sander."

He looks at me and asks: "Will you come back when he dies?" My entire body is shaking when I tell him about my decision to stay here, on the island. Jorn doesn't say anything for a while. "He would like you to be there for the cremation."

"I know. We talked about that right before I left. It's really difficult. I haven't yet made up my mind. Does Sander already want me to come back now?"

Jorn takes a minute to think about that. "No, at least he hasn't told me so. He's so tired he can't even think about whether you should come back or not." He gives me a hard look. "If I were you I'd come back for the cremation, Lide. I know he would really like that. It would be kind of weird, wouldn't it, if the love of his life isn't there for his farewell service?"

I notice the underlying tone of frustration in his voice and calmly answer: "I understand that and I appreciate you telling me how you feel. And God, I'd really like to be there to support you. But... I have to do this my way. If I fly back now I will probably never return to Hawaii. And here I will be able to say goodbye to him in my own way, to grieve and make a new start."

We're interrupted by my friend Saar who wants to Facetime, so Jorn and I quickly say goodbye with a virtual kiss. As soon as her big caring eyes appear on the screen, I feel an immense peace come over me. She's like a mother figure, who comforts me while softly rocking me. She was also a big support for Sander. They'd send each other long e-mails about their deepest fears and the beautiful moments in life.

"Hi, sweetie,' I hear her soft voice. "How are you?"

"I'm okay." But I can't hold back the tears any longer. "Sorry, Saar. I was just speaking to Jorn about Sander. I know Sander's not doing well at all. I'm pretty shaken up by that." Almost 7500 miles away, things stay silent for a while.

"Sweetie-pie, wouldn't you rather come back? You've got a good travel insurance, don't you? So that you can return to Hawaii after saying goodbye to Sander?" Again, silence. My head is completely empty and I don't manage to come up with an answer. "I'm just not sure, Saar. The flight here was so incredibly difficult. I felt sick to my stomach and was torn by grief for two days straight. I don't think I can go through that again."

She looks at me. "I understand that."

At that moment Bob walks by and greets me cheerfully. "And a wonderful Aloha-Friday to you." When he sees the sadness on my face the corners of his mouth immediately go down. He gives me an encouraging pat on the shoulder and walks on.

"Hey Li, look who else I've got here at the table," Saar says, turning the camera on her phone to show me. I see the mass of curls of her boyfriend Mels. Next to him is one of Sander's other best friends, In-soo. "Liedje dear, we love you," he shouts, taking a swig of beer. And then Saar is back again. "We've just said goodbye to Sander and are washing away our grief with wine and beer." It's good to see our friends get together in difficult times such as these. Oh, how I wish I could be there to hold them. "You can always call us if you want to talk, okay? Even if it's in the middle of the night. You know that, right?"

After we say goodbye I immediately put on my running gear. I have to get myself together to be able to decide what I should do. I leave the property and turn onto a steep tarmac road. Finding the straight road kind of boring, I decide to climb over a fence with a red sandy track behind it. I ignore the sign with PRIVATE PROPERTY in big red letters and run into the unspoiled jungle of Big Island. The path is flanked by passion fruit plants heavy with purple flowers as big as my hand entwined around the branches of mango trees. The natural beauty lifts my mood and the veil in my head, and I am able to think a bit more clearly.

I have to stay here, I know that. If I'd choose to leave now and fly back to The Netherlands, Sander would probably already be dead by the time I get there. Big Island's natural environment is the best place for me to cope with my grief. But my decision does feel ambivalent. There's nothing I'd rather do than be there for Sander during his last hours, but I also know he's not really there anymore and he might not even realize that I'd be there, or wouldn't be able to let go for fear of hurting me. A huge truck suddenly appears at the end of the rutted road. It's too late to dive into the bushes because the driver will surely have also seen me by now. I notice a big dog running next to the truck. I bet it's an aggressive pit bull with sharp teeth – they're very popular among the locals.

The driver stops, opens the door to let the dog in and then continues to drive towards me with considerable speed. I straighten up, preparing to "turn on my cutest smile" as Sander would put it. When the truck pulls up next to me, I step back. The man is stocky, just like his pit bull, and regards me with an inquisitive stare. "This is private property, would you please leave the premises as soon as possible?"

On the left side behind the truck I see a camper, an exact copy of the vehicle chemistry teacher Walter White from *Breaking Bad* uses to produce crystal meth. I point towards the fence, a quarter of a mile behind me, mumbling "sorry, I'm already gone," and quickly start running.

The man follows me in his truck and waits until I'm on the other side of the fence to make sure the gate is shut properly. Before walking back to his monster truck he greets me in the traditional Hawaiian way: a rapid shake of a balled fist with your pinky finger and thumb stretched out. I respond in kind and head back home to the safe haven of the Hawaiian Sanctuary.

Thirty minutes later I'm telling Bob about my recent adventure. "I don't think you've just run into a drug baron, it's more likely it was a security guard," he responds. "There's several American movie stars living on Big Island and their villas are well-protected."

I look at him. "How do you know that? Do you happen to know them personally?"

Bob straightens in his chair. "Yes, as a matter of fact I do, but I'm not allowed to talk about it." He motions as if he's closing a lock on his mouth. Slightly disappointed I walk towards the wooden counter between the kitchen and the lounge area and take a heart-shaped piece of raw chocolate from a little basket. I've momentarily managed to leave what's happening at home behind me but as soon as I turn on the Wi-Fi and the messages from home start pouring in, reality hits me in the face.

"Lide, I'm worried about you, will you please read my e-mail," Juuls asks. Should I? Just when I've managed to pick up the pieces and kind of feel okay again? Curiosity gets the better of me and I open my hotmail account.

Dear Liedje,

Like I said, I'm worried about you. I sometimes fear that you will regret not being there to say goodbye. I know this may sound contradictory to what I told you before, but that's because I understand what you're doing. But at the same time I really just want to have you here near me. So that I can see for myself how you're doing. Sometimes it feels like you've left your life here behind you. It's almost as if life here in Holland isn't real anymore. I don't know how else to describe it.

I'm very, very sad and I want to share that with you. You're choosing your own path to deal with all of this, to handle it. To handle life. But everything is connected. Your world over there, our world here. It all belongs to the same world. Sorry, I know I'm not helping by sending you this e-mail. But this is how I feel right now. Confused.

I love you
   Juuls

I pop the rest of the chocolate heart in my mouth. I have to let this sink in. Within a minute a new e-mail, this time from Saar, plops into my mailbox.

Dear Li,

I know how frightened you are and I understand you can't face getting on that plane right now, but think of all the terrible things you've managed to overcome these past years. This is the grand finale, this is the end of this earthly life. No one can imagine what you must be going through right now. But don't forget that we're here for you. Together we stand strong, like we've been doing all those years, together with you two. I've been rereading old e-mails in which Sander says how proud he is of you and wouldn't know what he would do without you.

It's so awful you not being there with him, precisely at this moment that must be so terribly scary for him. I can't imagine how it must be for you and Sander, but it feels awful that you're so far away.

E-mail is such a bad way of conveying these kinds of emotions, but it is also this medium that has made our friendship so much more beautiful these past years. We wrote each other at the craziest times. Often when we felt alone and felt the need to share our emotions and feelings, the bad ones and the good ones.

The moment that Sander won't be sending me such messages anymore is getting near, and I always looked forward to those e-mails of his. They were always a sign of life, hope and friendship. The time to say goodbye is getting closer. And I too need you. We need you. To be able to end this properly. You can only do that once, Li!

Please know that I'm not cornering you. I love you and you're very dear to my heart. It's just impossible to see Sander go without you. Every day you not being here feels less and less okay. I understand very, very well why you left, but I'm so incredibly scared that you will come to regret this.

Big kiss,
Saar

Doubt hits me like a bombshell now that both Juuls and Saar have written me the same kind of message. Sander needs me. How I wish I could hold his hand now and whisper sweet words into in his ear. I notice that my breathing is accelerating and my finger tips are starting to tingle. I know this feeling: it's a sure sign I'm starting to hyperventilate, just like what happened on the flight from Holland. The thought that I couldn't just get off the plane practically caused me to faint.

No. No. No. I can't do it, I'm not going to manage to spend another two days in a cramped aircraft suffering from anxiety and immense sadness. And I certainly won't be able to fly back to Hawaii afterwards, with Sander's emaciated and dying body embedded in my mind. My head empties out like a burst balloon and all my thoughts judder to a halt. My mind glazes over.

I feel Kalani's soft nose nudging my right ankle, right on the spot of the naupaka flower tattoo. I straighten up, pat the dog's shiny black fur and feel a surge of adrenalin flow through my body, almost like a rekindled fire. Could that be Pele's energy that Bob talked about? My intuition tells me I should stay on Big Island so that I can work through the pain of losing Sander in my own way and at my own pace. It's not an inner voice telling me what to do. It's actually a physical sensation. When I make the right decision I feel a warm flow in my stomach. When I make the wrong one I feel a tightness rising up to my throat.

"I'm so, so sorry that I can't be with you guys, dear Sander, Juuls and Saar. But I have to choose what's right for me, otherwise I won't survive this," I mumble in a soft voice.

I can't go back to my apartment in Utrecht, where all the memories are still way too fresh. Besides, after the cremation, everyone will go on with their lives, while I'll stay behind on my own. Too ill to look for a job or to return to Hawaii. Kalani tilts her little head towards me and snuggles up to my leg. I take out my iPad to distract myself with some music and I end up with the video clip of Maaike Ouboter's song "That I Miss You", the one that Sander wanted me to listen to when we said goodbye. My finger is trembling when I click "play" and listen to the lyrics. Yes, this time I do listen to them.

You kiss me, you hush me
Embrace me and shush me
You catch me, you crave me
And infinitely unscare me
You call me, you hear me
You save and upset me
Believe me, deprive me
And smother and stun me
You breathe and you live me
You shiver and shake me
You trust me
You consider me a person
And prevent me from heated dreams
That rise to the surface
The lonely questions of finite joy

With your curls like the night
The way you talk, the way you smile
Your voice, so close by
Soothingly soft like an angel's
In my dreams
the endless empty spaces flow
You slow me, you tame me
You touch me, you move me

I miss you, I miss you
I grab you, I grip you
I want you, I play you
I move and instruct you
To stay with me
During the dark nights
To no longer ache
For you

I smothered you, I froze you
I liberated and lost you
To a different place, but I still hear you
I embrace you, I warm you
I see and I feel you
I caress and I stroke you
I cuddle and hug you
You mature me, you get me
Yet you confuse and delude me
Sometimes it scares me
That I'm so much like you now
In my smile, in my tears
In my love of life
Forgive me for everything
Help me now, liberate me
And let me go
I can do this alone
But please hold me when I need you to
In your thoughts
And I see you everywhere around me
And although I sometimes think this is for the better
I can't help but miss you

I kiss you and hush you,
I douse and quench you
You remain very close
But in my head you're at rest.

Sometimes it's almost as if Sander was already gone these last few months. As if he already had one foot in the other world, to prepare himself *and* me for what was to come. He also knows we've got to let each other go, but it is so terribly difficult.

"But you can do it. By yourself. Just like I can," I sob quietly, hugging Kalani tightly to me. "Let go, sweetie, and come to me here. Embrace me in your thoughts, because I miss you so and I have to do the impossible: I have to let you go."

19   No more secrets

I'm chopping up unripe papayas with brute force. Sweat is pouring down my nose, down my neck and down my back. J. gives me a dubious sideways glance. He's looking remarkably casual today with his linen pants and white shirt; much more attractive than with those Arab outfits of his.

We've been doing overtime because of a workshop where participants are learning how to build and manage a self-sustaining farm. Our challenge is to provide these American, Australian and Norwegian mouths - thirty people in total - with three meals a day. In between my chores I sometimes pop into a lecture and manage to pick up a thing or two. For instance I now know that Big Island is not only the most isolated archipelago in the world but also has the purest oxygen and rainwater on the whole planet. The island counts no less than seven climate zones, which explains the unsurpassable diversity of flora and fauna. The contrast between the tropical East and dry West is inconceivably large.

J. and I decide to take a break to treat ourselves to some fresh coconut water. I ask him how he ended up on Big Island.

"My fiancée wanted to live and work here," is his succinct answer.

"So she's also going to come here?" I ask, curious.

He lowers his head and softly says: "She died of breast cancer a couple of months ago."

I cover my mouth with my hand. "Oh, how terrible, but

how good of you to come here all the same," I add encouragingly, looking at his sun-tanned face. His voice is calm and composed when he continues: "I wanted to experience this for the both of us, the natural world and the power of the island. I will be leaving for Paris in a couple of months. I'm going to study at the Film Academy and master the French language, the language my girlfriend was fluent in."

J. turns to me with an inquisitive look on his face. "And how did you end up on Big Island?"

Since he's been so candid I don't want to hold back. "We share the same kind of grief." I decide to tell him everything: about the last five years of Sander's illness, about the fact that he will probably die very soon and about my decision to stay here.

He doesn't say anything and although I'm expecting a lack of understanding and disdain, instead I see a look of compassion and acknowledgement on his face. Without hesitating he approaches me and embraces me. He holds me without saying anything and I realize how badly I've missed someone touching me. "Nobody can know what you're going through," J. whispers.

We spend the rest of the afternoon preparing the most beautiful dishes. Wraps made out of heart-shaped hibiscus leaves filled with an avocado-walnut cream, sweet potato with crunchy bits of bell pepper, pumpkin soup with papaya garnished with edible purple passion fruit flowers, and pure dark chocolate mousse with macadamia nuts and mint leaves. Meanwhile we listen to J.'s playlist, which features Israel Kamakawiwo'ole's *Somewhere over the Rainbow* several times. Everyone ends up singing along at the top of their voice.

At 7 p.m. I collapse on my bed. What a day! We started at eight this morning cleaning the yoga area and we just ended with a huge pile of dirty dishes. Thank God the Hawaiian Sanctuary does have washing machines. I lie there staring up at the big tree in front of the jungalow with branches that must be at least 65 feet wide. When the swinging door opens I see it's Akiko quietly sneaking into our cabin. I lift my head to greet her. "Hi! Don't worry, I'm awake." She comes over and sits down on my bed.

"Are you okay?" she asks, with a worried look on her face. I really don't want to be "the-poor-girl-with-the-sick-boyfriend-that-everyone-feels-sorry-for", like I am back home, but after confiding in J. I can no longer keep my emotions to myself. Akiko edges closer to me and puts her arm around my shoulder. She sits next to me without saying anything. She comforts me without words, just like J. did. She leaves it up to me whether I want to say anything and when. At some point she moves behind me and places her hands on my shoulders. "Relax. I will give you a *lomi lomi* massage."

The heat from her hands flows through my shoulders to my arms, my stomach and my legs. It's a deep Reiki treatment, just like I used to give Sander. Her tender, loving touch breaks down the emotional walls I've built around myself and the bitter feeling of loneliness is replaced by a strong sense of connection. Why did I try so hard to keep everyone out these past weeks? Because this feels so much better. When Akiko is finished she hugs me and holds me for several minutes. Her quiet breathing and silence relaxes me.

Later that evening I Skype with my mom. Together with my brothers and sisters-in-law she'd said goodbye to Sander today. For thirteen years they treated Sander like a son and brother. The tears in her eyes immediately tell me she's really upset but is trying to put on a brave face for me. "He's really spent, Liedje. His body is so fragile," she says. "I sat with him for a while and kept his lips moist." We are now both crying. "He told your sisters-in-law, Irene and Mariël, they should shine.

Isn't that something?!"

I know he always worried about the girls. Sander thought they were too caught up in their heads. "They need to seriously let their hair down," he'd concluded one day. "Dancing the night away with a few cocktails. That's just how it works."

Despite my tears I have to laugh. "Oh, typical Sander! He wants to give them a valuable message." And then I'm suddenly overwhelmed by fatigue. "Mom, I really have to go to bed now." She smiles an understanding and nurturing smile like only a mother can.

Back in the jungalow I immediately fall asleep and slip into a life-like dream.

It's my dad! He's staring at a large hole in the ground. He kneels down by the edge and leans forward while a white light illuminates his wrinkleless features. He reaches out and pulls someone through the hole towards him. *It's Sander!* I sit up with a start; it's like someone has just given me a jolt of 220 volt.

Right before my father passed away I'd asked him: "Will you take care of Sander when it's time? Will you help him, when he's left this world?" The moment I've been dreading for the past five years has arrived. Sander is going to leave this world.

20 Without Sander

 Jorn:
"Hi Lide, our friend Sander passed away this morning. He's gone. It's alright now. x"

I sink to the ground, shaking all over while staring at the screen of my iPhone. My Sander, the love of my life, my everything is no longer here. His heart, the spot where I'd always place my hand right before we fell asleep, is no longer beating.

Panic and a sense of peace. I'm overwhelmed by two completely different emotions, simultaneously, full-blown and involuntary. Panic: I will never again be able to talk to Sander, to hold him, to kiss him. Peace: I now know he's finally free of his fears and that terribly sick body. For a brief moment I actually dare to hope these two extremes will bless my mind with a strange sort of balance, but no. I've completely lost all sense of balance; literally and figuratively, because I can't even walk. Paralyzed by the news I remain there on the floor for quite some time, gently rocking back and forth. "I'm so incredibly proud of you, San. You dared to let go of life. Will you come here to me now?"

When I've kind of gotten myself back together I call Jorn, glad that he immediately answers.

"Hi, Lide. It's happened. The GP gave him a sedative last night, hoping that he would go quietly in his sleep. And that's how it happened." His voice sounds unsteady. "The cremation will probably be next week."

We're both shattered and at a loss for words so we agree

to talk later that day. I call my mother, text a few friends of mine and after that I walk straight back to the jungalow where I curl up under the covers. I wish I could disappear. Biting into the pillow I shout as loud as I can without anyone hearing it. Worn-out from all the thoughts and emotions I stare at the long shadows of the palm trees. I feel a slight pressure, as if two hands are stroking my face. I jack-knife upright in bed. "Is that you, San?" I ask, startled. "Are you here with me?"

No answer.

At 7 o'clock I'm wide awake and again immediately sit up straight. This is the first day of the rest of my life without Sander. I've so often tried to imagine this moment. I'd walk through downtown Utrecht, imagining Sander had just died and that I would now have to go on by myself. I'd jump on my bike and rush back home, back to him. The real thing feels like there's a metal armor wrapped around my wrenched body. The Japanese girls are still asleep when I tiptoe outside and see Maura's meditation class is about to start.

"Aloha!" she cries out energetically. She's American, she's beautiful *and* she has the longest eyelashes I've ever seen. Like the rest of the group I sit down in lotus position. Maura asks us to set an intention or, like they say in Hawaii, a "manifestation". "You could for instance ask for a beautiful miracle today," she explains.

I ask for strength and let that word circle through my mind like a mantra. *Strength. Strength... Strength...*

And then everyone practically jumps up because the room is suddenly filled with ear-splittingly loud Argentine tango music. We look at each other with nervous smiles. Maura walks toward the audio equipment with a perplexed look on her face. "I don't get it. This is not my music and besides, I haven't even plugged in my iPod yet."

This is it! This is Sander's sign. I immediately remember our talk and the deal we made. He'd said: "When I've arrived safely I will give you a sign by suddenly turning on music."

Maura is elated when I tell her the story. "That certainly is a sign!" She hugs me.

The news spreads like wildfire and at breakfast everyone gives me a supportive aloha-cuddle. Anna, one of the teachers from Australia, hugs me closely. Her nickname is "Mother Nature", because she knows absolutely everything there is to know about plants and trees. She was the one who convinced me to come to Big Island when I saw her in the video on the website of the Hawaiian Sanctuary, where she talked about Pele's power.

"*Hya*, Lide," she says, pressing her thin body firmly against mine. "I dreamt there was an incredible energy shift around you. Did you happen to feel anything?"

I tell her about Sander's passing. She stays silent for a moment and then says, in a very firm voice: "Today we are going to take care of *you*. Take it easy and be ready after dinner. We're going to have ourselves some beers in Pahoa!"

I smile at her plan. "That would have been Sander's idea exactly!"

She gives me a kiss and a loving pat on the head. I'm so glad this lady is going to take care of me.

That evening we drive to a bar in Pahoa, which is only a couple of miles away, in a car with monstrously large tires. Anna orders several hefty pints of Longboard beer, a specialty from neighboring island Maui. She turns to me and the others who've come along and says: "Cheers to Sander and cheers to Lide!"

We toast. "Here's to our life, San!" I say, looking up at the heavens.

Later that evening, back at the Sanctuary, Anna escorts

me to the yoga area which has been transformed into a lounge with music, colored lights, candles, incense and, right in the middle of the room, a big pile of cushions in the shape of a bird. "Would you please lie down right there?" she asks, winking. All the workshop participants are already there and they encourage me to lie down. "Go on then, Lide." Bob is sitting on the floor, next to the bird, and swings his arms to and fro in a welcoming gesture. I walk up to him, kneel down on the cushions, close my eyes and wait. When I feel two hands stroke my stomach I freeze. It's Kim, one of the participants. "Does this hurt, right here?" With a flat hand she makes a rotating movement. I nod. That spot feel very tense indeed.

"Sigh very deeply a couple of times," she instructs me. When I exhale she rubs the blockage downwards and out of my body. It's almost like it's a modern version of an ancient ritual, with tribe members performing a healing. On my head, my toes and my arms I feel simultaneous stroking motions of several hands. They're giving me a lomi lomi group massage! Because of all the loving strokes I can no longer hold back the sadness. I don't want to but I start to cry with great heaving sobs and convulsive gasps. Snot and tears are streaming down the sides of my face, staining the pillows. In a flash I suddenly see Sander behind the turntables, in front of a large crowd of people who are yelling. He's looking for me. I wave and our eyes lock. We both laugh. "Let go, let go," Anna cries out, followed by a deep sigh. I do the same and feel an intense relaxed feeling come over me. Anna and Bob are beating on a drum while making hula dance-like leaps around me. "Haaaaa... Ha..." Anna exhales again. The pain in my heart is transformed into a childlike joy. This is crazy! What is happening? Would Sander now laugh just as loud as I am?

That night I wake up with a start. Next to my bed I see a green pulsating light. Slightly panicked I switch on the light.

Nothing. I lie down on my back and feel the powerful beating of my heart. What was that? Sander? "How are you?" I whisper, closing my eyes. "Don't just go and appear out of nowhere and scare me to death, okay?"

Nothing. But later that night we meet up in a dream. "How are you?" I look at his loving eyes that I'm so familiar with.

"Fine, just a bit tired." He strokes my cheek with the back of his hand. "You know I love you, don't you?" I give a small nod and take his hand. "I love you too. I love you so much!"

21   No contact

"STOOOOOOP!!!!" That's what the capital letters on the screen of my iPhone say. It's Sander's mothers reply to my text in which I share my grief with them. It's clear that she wants nothing to do with me since I didn't come to his deathbed and won't be going to the cremation either. I feel a painful stab in my stomach. This is the inevitable consequence of my decision. In my last phone call with Sander's sister a few days ago it became quite clear his family doesn't ever want to see me again. We did discuss his last wishes for the farewell ceremony and talked it all over: about Sander wanting to choose the music himself, that he was focused on organizing the after party with his best friends and that he wanted them to eat, dance and especially drink until the early hours. Everyone had to go "loesoe" - in other words, he wanted it to be a blowout of a party. We would break a taboo.

I once read in a research article that no more than one in five people dare to talk about the dying process itself. What Sander found especially difficult about the whole thing was that I and his family and friends would stay behind grief-stricken. He had more or less accepted his own fate, living on with all those ailments was no longer doable.

I reread Sander's mothers text. Is this really going to be the last thing she says to me? For thirteen years I was part of their family, which included two brothers and a younger sister. Because of his illness we became a lot closer, but does it really mean our bond is gone now that's gone? Everything gone just like that? I do understand why they want to break with me and why they disapprove of my decision. Even my own mother finds it difficult to come to terms with that, so imagine how they must be feeling... My thoughts drift off and I remember the talk I had with my family before I decided to leave for Big Island.

The sun illuminates the faces of my mother, my two brothers, my sisters-in-law and my three-year old nephew.

"Daan?" I inquire when the little guy runs op to me. "Why don't you find us a good place to sit?" He takes my hand, resolutely pulling me towards the sandy path up the hill. "Here, aunty Li," he says, sitting down on a patch of very soft moss. We form a circle and sit down just like we did when we said goodbye to my father. We take each other's hand but this time our thoughts are focused on Sander. Together we send him extra strength to help him through this difficult period. We know from experience how effective that can be. A few days before we left for our trip to the US and Hawaii, Sander came down with severe pneumonia. It looked like our dream trip would go up in smoke. I'd just read about how mind power works and decided to try it out so I asked friends and family to send Sander powerful thoughts at a certain time and to fervently wish he would get better. A few days later we were drinking champagne in the departure lounge at Schiphol Airport.

"I can see you," Daan reacts to our closed eyes. We all burst out laughing. My phone bleeps. It's a message from Sander, who's been staying at his parent's house.

Sander:

"Hi there sweetie, would you please ask your family how they feel about your decision to not be here should I happen to "go"? That you choose to create your own way to do that, from a distance? To be honest, I would really like you to be there, for you to be sitting near me at an angle so that I can look at you. Of course I respect your decision, but I'm really struggling with the whole thing and think I'm slowly starting to form an opinion about it. I'm just really curious to know what your "crew" thinks. Big kiss."

Choked up I manage to pass Sander's question on to my family and see their expressions darken with worry. "So what do you think about my decision?"

My mother wipes away her tears with a handkerchief. "I find it very difficult, Liedje. It must be terribly hard for Sander to leave without the person dearest to his heart. I'm also afraid your trip is a flight out of fear and that you will come to regret this immensely."

These past months I've been over and over that scenario in my head, but a very strong gut feeling tells me I have to go. I sigh deeply and silently stare at a long-haired cow that languidly stares back at me. "I really feel I should go, mom. My body and my spirit are completely empty. Completely spent."

In a flash I suddenly see Sander's emaciated body in front of me. His mind is unreachable, just like it used to be during those feverish trips that I have become all too familiar with. I see myself sitting beside the bed, with his hand in mine. The

122

small hands of the clock are moving excruciatingly slowly, ticking away his last hours, announcing the final blow.

The images of that talk with my family is replaced by a different one: my walks through the forest with Sander's mother. We shared our grief but also tried to find solutions for the awful situation at hand. We were both distraught about Sander's excessive drinking. When he was at his worst, the only ones Sander allowed near him were me and his parents, which is why we became so close.

Without them there I would surely have collapsed from the strain. And that's what makes this abrupt break extra painful. Yet I understand that they've come to this decision because they don't approve of the fact that I have chosen to not be there during those very last weeks of Sander's life. I can't imagine how difficult it must have been for his family, to see that last bit of remaining life force flow out of him.

22 Star of the Sea Painted Church

Do not seek fame,
do not make plans.
Do not lose yourself in activities.
Do not think you know everything.

Embrace everything that crosses your path
and avoid set paths.
Embrace what heaven has given you
but know you possess nothing.
Be empty.
Completely empty.

The perfect man uses his mind like a mirror,
welcoming nothing, refusing nothing,
reflecting everything and holding nothing.

Tswang Tse

"'Enjoy with a capital E," I mumble softly into the tear-soaked pillow. Sander considered that a terribly snooty remark, but did end up making it his motto. I curl up into a fetal position, trying to find shelter and a way to end this gut-wrenching feeling of loneliness. The love of my life made every day into a party, no matter how miserable he was feeling. Whenever I got up on the wrong side of the bed he would sing songs he made up himself or he'd manage to get me out of one a dark mood by pulling a silly face.

"I will never be able to laugh with you again," I whisper softly.

Sander could turn a depressing Monday into a culinary feast: with shrimp cocktails, and greasy mackerel and salmon from the fishmonger. *And* a bottle of Moët & Chandon, even if he had to face wintery snow flurries to walk to the liquor store. We will never ever again eat fresh fried fish together.

He downloaded series like *Homeland* and *Dexter* and we'd watch episode after episode, tightly snuggled up on the couch. For Sander enjoying himself was not limited to time, regimen or budget.

I've lost you.

Again I bury my head in the pillow and shout as loud as I can. This is my pain pillow; it's been five days since Sander died and I miss him so. Grief sweeps through me like waves, comes out in a waterfall of tears, leaving behind a terrible emptiness.

I am however getting better in managing to deal with my emotions. As soon as I feel a new wave coming on I retreat to an old tree at the back of the property to feel through them. Sometimes I sit there for minutes on end in silence. Meditating brings anger and fear to the surface, but I don't fight my emotions and instead listen to the messages they contain. I know that underneath anger and despair is sadness. And by acknowledging it, it loses its power and sharpness.

I want to say goodbye to Sander today; I just haven't yet figured out where I want to do that. And so I just wait and see what comes up. Meanwhile I put a candle, a lighter and incense in my purse so that I will be prepared when the special moment does manifest itself.

I try to pep myself up by telling myself it's time for a shower.

With my nightshirt still on I walk towards the yoga area where there's two outdoor communal showers. On the way there I pick a flower shaped like a pinecone. The gooey liquid that drips from the bottom is the best natural soap in the world. I also strip a couple of small leaves of the Katuk plant for my daily dose of calcium as well as vitamin A, B1 and C. I nibble at it; it tastes slightly sweetened and it's extremely addictive and yummy.

The place is deserted, safe for a few chickens with white feathered legs pottering about. It's ten a.m. and with the sun already high in the clear blue sky it's over 77 degrees in the shade.

I drape my towel over the wooden door, get in under the rain shower and lather up with the scentless stuff from the flower bud. I take a deep breath of fresh morning air and look at how the soft breeze makes the tufts of palm tree foliage look like dancing hula skirts. The smell of the wet earth reminds me of the Tropical Pavilion at Burgers' Zoo in the city of Arnhem, where Sander and I once went. I also recognize the strong spicy undertone. *Hey, wait a minute...* That's weed! Someone is smoking a joint. I quickly dry off, put some light summer clothes on and decide to go and investigate. Following the smoke I soon end up at the toilet block right next to the showers. And there I see the chicken catcher, leaning on his bike, with a joint as thick as a temaki sushi. The man with the bushy eyebrows is halfway his sixties and is taking a long, slow drag, holding the smoke in his lungs for a bit, and then exhales excruciatingly slowly. The smoke drifts off towards the basket on his bike, where I see several motionless fluffy chicks staring into space. They must be high as hell.

I don't want to disturb him and walk on towards the complementary bikes. I decide to take the "beach cruiser" that also has a little flag. I hop on and head for the beach - a downhill ride of about three miles. The speed and the wind in my hair feels lovely and I try hard not to think about the way back, because I will never manage to get back up the hill. The green thicket of trees flanking the road gradually makes way for a more open landscape with palm trees. Straight ahead of me I see the black lava plain and the green-blue ocean. The break pad squeaks when I see an abandoned church and decide to slow down. I cautiously stick my head around the pastel green door but there's no one in sight. I let my eyes slide over the colorful collection of paintings on the wall. Every inch of the wooden panels is filled with depictions of angels and Jesus and Mary, but I also see the lava plains of Big Island and a white man with a long beard. A handwritten text tells me that's the Belgian missionary Evarist Gielen, who built this Star of the Sea Painted Church in 1927. The church was moved in the nineties, when a lava stream came dangerously close and threatened to destroy it. I sit down on a wooden bench near the altar and stay there for a while, staring at a painting of a dark-skinned woman with a baby, surrounded by angels.

"Aloha," I greet her politely, "would you perhaps be able to send someone who can take me home? *Mahalo!*"

The sea breeze through the open windows plays with the blonde locks of my hair before disappearing through the windows on the other side. I just sit there, staring into space, feeling detached. I don't feel anything. No sadness, no despair, no loss. When I get back on my bike a little later I'm surprised by the silence I experienced within myself. It was almost like a hole in time, a sort of empty space between past and present or, to put it more simply, it felt like the Now.

The wind takes me along further downhill in the direction of Pele's playground, with young palm trees and big rocks of solidified lava. I buy two cans of cool beer at a small shop, lock my bike and head for the sea. Sitting underneath a small palm tree I light the purple candle, open the beer and take a swig of the dark ale. "Sweetie, San!" I shout towards the ocean. "I love you with my whole heart and soul. Even though we couldn't be together during that last period, you are and will always be my everything. We became adults together and our lives will forever be interwoven. It's no coincidence that the legend of the naupaka flower crossed your path, because that's how you set out a new path for me. I realize that now, now that I'm here at the foot of Fire Goddess' Pele's volcano! The *now* is *everything!*"

A car pulls up next to me. "Do you need a ride?" the driver asks me. "Oh, yes! That would be great!" I'm thrilled *and* bathing in sweat due to several attempts to cycle up the hill in the scorching sun. He deposits my muddy bike on the spotless white leather upholstery and gives me a friendly handshake. "Aloha, I'm Josef."

23   Light switch *on*

Ika Pono Mea
(All is perfect)

Aunty Mahealani

An old rusty car is making its way up the dirt track. Kalani runs up to the vehicle barking furiously while trying to bite the back left tire.

"Kalani!" shouts J. from the doorstep of the kitchen. "Come over here, you crazy animal!" He shoos her away towards a couple of chickens scratching at the dirt. The dog goes out of its way to avoid them because she's terrified of the fluffy monsters. Every morning they invariably steal her dog food and as soon as the first chicken approaches the bowl Kalani skulks away to hide under the couch.

It's two p.m. and I can feel the sun burning my skin. The Puna jungle is a wonderful place to live with its thousands of flowers and the veggies and fruit fresh off the land, but working here is a different matter. I'm not used to the sweltering heat and during the day I'm like a vampire, running from one shady spot to the next, afraid my skin might melt.

With the attention and patience of a Buddhist I sweep the floors of the three buildings on the property. The lounge is my favorite area: it's the only place with Wi-Fi and thus my connection to the outside world, with my friends and my family who support me in my grieving process, and I them.

I watch how the car lurches towards the parking lot, trying to avoid the many rain puddles. An older woman with a wreath of red flowers in her silver-grey hair gets out. There's no mistaking her, that *has* to be Aunty Mahealani. This Hawaiian lady is a bit of a celebrity in the Puna District, the region where I now live. Under the name of Kumu 'Elele 'O Na Kupuna she travels all over the island to spread Hawaiian wisdom and messages. She's quite a striking figure and so is the woman at her side, who also has a a beautiful flower wreath in her hair. She turns out to be Aunty's apprentice and is learning how to become a "kumu", the Hawaiian word for "spiritual teacher". Both women are able to channel information and messages from ancestors. With a healthy dose of humor they are able to connect our earthly life with the spirit world, says Bob when he introduces them.

Today they've come to teach us about Hawaiian traditions and rituals. I'm desperate for some kind of message from Sander, but immediately try to stifle that hope because I don't want to be disappointed. I quickly sweep the last bits of dust off the stone floor, put the broom away, splash some water over my face and install myself on the soft cushions of the wicker couch.

Aunty places a rough rock crystal as big as my forearm on the table in front of her. "Don't be shy now. Feel free to put it on your lap if you want to. He *loves* that," she jokes.

Our eyes meet and I can't help but think there's a mysterious glint in hers. Her eyes are both dark and light, but without a sparkle or anything dark, as if present in absence. Who is hiding behind those unfathomable eyes? I'd love to bombard Aunty with questions, but decide to keep my distance for now. I carefully pick up the enormous crystal and place it in my lap to examine it. It's long and slender and is a bit thicker at the top. Wait a minute... It's a phallus. I might actually be holding the largest crystal in the world and it just happens to look like a penis. How totally bizarre!

Aunty begins as soon as everyone is seated. She turns out to be a practiced performer. "Aloooooha! Why don't you tell me a bit about yourselves first? What brings you here, to Big Island?" Her mysterious eyes sweep over the circle of people in front of her and stop at Turiya. "Would you like to begin?" Turiya is sitting next to me and I can tell she's nervous. She fidgets, kicks off her slippers and gets into lotus position.

"My son Baraka and I have been traveling and studying with various teachers and shamans from around the world. We were brought to Hawaii to help establish a retreat center in Waipio Valley. I am grateful to now be getting certified in permaculture here at the Hawaiaan Sanctuary, to deepen our harmonious connection to the land and culture, while also building my own business."

"Oh yes. This is indeed the right place," says Aunty, with a sparkle in her eyes. "For everyone sitting here now it's the right spot. It's no coincidence that you are here on the island. It's part of the bigger picture; think of it that way." She explains that because of the volcanic activity Big Island has a sort of explosive power, which affects the people living on the island. "Emotions are first brought to the surface and then swept away, just like a smoldering lava stream destroys everything on its path. We call Big Island "the Healing Island", but be careful, it can be very intense. If you happen to fly into a rage or feel terribly sad, it's best to allow those emotions. Just let it be and don't push it. That's the best way to survive this island."

Kim raises her hand, slides to the edge of her chair and tucks her blond hair behind her ear with her index finger. Her friend, Rosin, is sitting next to her. She's blonde, Norwegian, an Olympic snowboard champion and very stylishly dressed in a dark blue skirt and a thin white T-shirt. Kim in contrast seems to go for the tough look, with her checkered blouse, denim shorts and a straw cowboy hat.

"Do you have a question?" Aunty asks.

The blond woman nods. "I was on Big Island a few years ago and felt very unsettled then. I couldn't sleep because my body was too agitated and after a week I decided to fly back home. This time things are very different; I feel calm."

Aunty smiles. "Big Island reinforces your emotional state. At that time you were apparently not yet ready for a visit to the island, but now the time is ripe." Aunty again looks around the circle, but this time sternly, with a very powerful look in her eyes. "Beware of the powers of this island," she warns us. "Be careful what you wish for. Make sure your intentions and thoughts are clear, because they might just be fulfilled."

"And you? Why have you come here?" She's turned to me with an innocent school girl look. I immediately feel myself blushing. "I'm here to work, but I also want to learn as much as possible about Hawaiian nature and culture," I begin hesitantly. Shall I tell her the whole story about Sander and the legend of Naupaka? Oh heck, why not. It takes me all of one minute to fill her in on my reasons for being here. "We were inseparable until the doctors told us they couldn't stop the cancer cells from growing. And that's how I ended up losing the love of my life." I tell them about the naupaka flower, about his drinking problem, that he passed away recently and that I'm hoping to meet him again, here, on Big Island.

Aunty's voice is soft when she answers. "Your feeling was correct. You belong here right now. Sander lost the connection with himself and could only re-find it by severing the connection between the two of you. He's here now."

"Really? Could I ask him something?" Aunty nods. "I would like to know if it was difficult for him to go to the other side, to let go of everything."

She doesn't say anything and cocks her head slightly as if

she's trying to pick up a sound.

"He says it went swiftly and easily, like switching on the light."

Turiya puts her hand on my knee and gently squeezes my leg. Aunty continues: "Here in Hawaii we call the transition to the spirit world 'a change of address'."

I start laughing. "Wow, that's beautiful! Is my dad with Sander? He died four months before Sander changed address."

"Yes, they're together," she answers resolutely. "Your father and your boyfriend already knew each other way before this earthly life, in another era, and they're now buddies in the light yet again." She pauses as if she's discussing something with her ancestors in the spirit world. She closes her eyes, nods and then continues: "You are going to write a book. And it's very important that you do that." All heads turn towards me, eagerly awaiting my reaction.

"But why?" I ask, surprised. She straightens up and gives me a piercing look. "To tell the world about the path you've chosen to follow and about the lessons you will learn here on Big Island."

J. puts his hand on my knee and turns to me with a beaming smile. "I would hereby like to order your first book."

More hands are raised. "Me too," says Turiya.

"And don't forget us," Kim adds.

I'm momentarily at a loss for words, not knowing what's hit me. "Do you think it will become a bestseller?" I ask, straight to the point.

"Would you want it to be?" Aunty's tone has become a tad cool. I realize it's a trick question and immediately feel guilty about my greediness.

"I would like to be able to tell as many people as possible about the lessons I've learned," I rephrase my remark, leaning back in the cushions as Aunty tells us about her own unexpected success when she started singing in a Hawaiian band.

"It started off as a joke and it ended with an album award," she concludes her story. She laughs exuberantly at her own memories and we all join in. She suddenly grows quiet and sticks her chin in the air. "Sander is coming through very strongly now. He wants me to tell you something." And then she pauses again while I eagerly await his message. "He's going to help you write it. He says you don't have to do it by yourself."

I'm baffled, because Sander always edited my articles and right before he died he urged me to write a book. And now all of a sudden the love of my life is with me and my goal is clear!

I'm a writer.

Light switch *on*

24 Sander?

If you've momentarily lost your way, trust the answer will come to you. Every day has its own worries, solutions and miracles.

Jesus in the Gospel of Thomas

Scrubbing toilets, sweeping out the yoga area and helping to cut up fruit and vegetables in the kitchen; after one and a half months the long work days are really starting to get to me. The muscles in my lower back are creaking in protest and there's a nerve in my foot sending out a constant, nagging pain. I take a look at myself in the mirror in the work-out room. Well, there's good news as well: my hair has become a lot blonder and my eyes look greener and brighter. The scales tell me I weigh 132 pounds which means I've lost 11 pounds in one month.

The workshop is over, the participants are gone and there's a distinct desolate feel about the place. In fact, it's deafeningly silent at the Hawaiian Sanctuary. I desperately try to get rid of the loneliness and feeling of emptiness by interacting with the people that are still there, but communicating is becoming increasingly difficult. For most of them English is their mother tongue, so they speak fairly quickly. I find talking is now sapping me of energy instead of giving me energy. I'm becoming more and more of a loner and am wracked by doubts and insecurity. Do people still like me? Do I still *want* to stay and work here? The maelstrom of thoughts is back. I look for distraction in the garden, where today I'm allowed to use brute force. With a razor-sharp machete I'm chopping dry leaves off a banana tree. They fall on to the ground with a hollow sound and soon a pathetic little stump with a huge bunch of bananas hanging from it is all that remains.

"Oh no!" I cry out. "I think I might have overdone it."

Coulter, one of the permanent staff members at the Hawaiian Sanctuary, looks at me and bursts out laughing. "Don't worry, that's just perfect." His beard is full of wood chips and his face is smeared with mud. On the surface he looks like any manual worker who knows what hard work is, but he's a very gentle soul and has been through quite a lot. Coulter lost his father to cancer and he now looks after his sick mother.

"You're a pretty strong lady," he now says. "I bet choosing to stay here was not easy."

I give him an aloha-hug to thank him for his support and register the mix of sweat, tobacco and mud on him. "You're quite tough yourself, mister."

I hear giggling and see the Japanese girls sitting at the bar in the lounge area chatting with Nathan, who practices *qigong,* a Chinese technique meant to cleanse the soul and open the heart. There's something weird about him, with his lanky hair that he wears loose one day only to tie it back in a samurai-like chignon the next. I prefer to keep my distance and that feeling seems to be mutual. But he's incredibly nice to Akiko and Maya. He pours them cups of tea, prepares herbal elixirs, and has given them a qigong healing by placing his hands on their head; an old Chinese technique for the exchange of energies. Meanwhile, he now and then glances at me with an almost envious look in his eyes. He reminds me of Sméagol in *The Lord of the Rings,* guarding his "precious" ring. But maybe I'm just imagining things because lately I've been having trouble distinguishing between what's real and not.

The boundaries between the two worlds - the terrestrial and the supernatural one - are blending together more and more often. For instance, I was talking to Sander only a couple of days ago. I was lying on the cedar wooden bench in the sauna when I suddenly heard someone call my name.

"Li!"

I jerk upright with a start and look around me. That sounded a lot like Sander. When I close my eyes I see his blue-gray eyes and heart-shaped lips and cropped hair.

"Is that you, San?" I inquire hesitantly.

"Who else would it be?" he reacts.

For a moment I wonder if I've gone crazy. Am I creating this voice in my head? But why would I want to call myself? And besides, the answers are coming more quickly than I could possibly think them up.

"If it's really you San, can you give me a sign?" I ask. Almost immediately I hear Michael Jackson's song Bad, with the word 'Shamone'. That used to be Sander's favorite stopgap. I bury all my doubts and ask him how he's doing.

"Really great! You might find it hard to believe, but I've got a turntable here and your dad frequently comes by to listen."

I hear his childlike, joyous laughter, like only Sander could laugh. "My dad?! You mean he's here as well?"

"No, no. He spends a great deal of time with your mother, to comfort her. He finds it very difficult that he can't contact her like we are able to, through music or like we're doing now. She thinks too much, which blocks the connection. She should start meditating in order to be able to meet up with him. Go ahead and tell her that." Sander also says I shouldn't be sad and should start living again. "Enjoy the island, Liedje. And take good care of yourself."

When I leave the spa I realize I have to share this with someone. With Turiya...? I find her staring at her laptop screen in the otherwise deserted lounge area. "Hi, Lide," she reacts, laughing at my flushed face. "Looks like you've been enjoying the sauna."

I toss my towel over the back of a chair and join her at the table. "Can I tell you about something really strange that just happened?" I ask tentatively. "It was really weird, just now in the sauna, and I'm not sure what to make of it."

She frowns, closes her laptop and straightens up, all ears. "Of course you may tell me. I'm listening."

I take a sip of water and suddenly wonder if I should... Maybe tomorrow everyone will be gossiping about "that girl from Holland who hears the voice of her dead boyfriend". But then I think 'oh, what the...' and decide to tell her anyway. When I'm finished Turiya has a look of surprise on her face. "See", I immediately think. How could I have been so stupid? "Think before you talk, Li!"

But then she says. "I know exactly what you mean. Or rather, the same thing happened to me with my father. He'd had a heart valve operation and was in a coma for a while. When he finally came out of that he was in very poor health. I was shattered when he died six months later. But he came to visit me, just like Sander just visited you. Initially I thought the same thing as you: that it was my own thoughts. Until my father told me things I couldn't possibly have known. At that point I realized our contact was not a figment of my imagination. Only after I let go of all my preconceived ideas about what is real and what not, and surrendered myself, trusting in the experience, I was able to 'understand' him very clearly. So dissolve your ego, Lide, and believe in this encounter."

I lean forward and embrace this kindred spirit with a

feeling of intense gratitude and relief.'

Not long after that Sander comes by again, this time when I'm sitting underneath an old tree, resting from an afternoon of back-breaking garden work. I've been working the hard, volcanic soil with a pickaxe to be able to plant seeds in it, which felt like I was working on my own soul - an empty space where new life is starting to sprout slowly but surely. I do really want to live a full life again, like Sander told me to, but I am not yet able to actually do it. The feeling of intense loss and sorrow are still too present to be able to go through life with a smile on my face.

Leaning against the tree trunk, I close my eyes and then suddenly Sander is sitting right next to me. He takes me by the hand.

"Ah, Liedje, Liedje... I'm doing fine. There's no need to cry."

I think of Turiya's words: let go of your perception of what reality is and believe. And so I say: "I miss you terribly, San."

He speaks to me like a wise teacher. "Listen, the two of us are now one single energy, so I'm always with you, wherever you are. You don't have to lead an isolated life anymore like we did all those years. I'm free now but so are you. So try to make the most of it because you still have so many great and magical moments to experience. Go for it, Li!"

I wipe away the tears and already feel a lot better. "Okay, San. From now on I will do things differently. Enjoy with a capital E!"

25 Cacao Ceremony

A shopping spree: I hardly dare to admit it, but I'm starting to crave one. I'm kind of fed up with the outfits in my backpack: three pairs of shorts, a few basic shirts, a black dress and a green vest. Tonight is the night of the Cacao Ceremony. There will be a party with dancing afterwards and I've got nothing to wear. Pouting, I stare at myself in the cracked mirror on the rickety wicker table in the jungalow. Because of the downpour last night everything in the cabin feels clammy. The rain water has even made its way through the concrete floor, forming a moist layer on all the blankets, pillows and clothes.

Yes, it's high time to go and splurge! And that is the end of the promise I made myself to refrain from spending money on my favorite hobby for two whole months.

"Enjoy," I recall Sander's words again, and yes, that's exactly what I'm going to do! I tie my blond hair into a high bun and admire the result in the mirror. Hm... I'm less pleased with my bangs. They're way too long, so I resolutely take out a pair of scissors and cut the ragged strands into a perfectly straight line. Thirty minutes later I'm cruising through the hippie-like town of Pahoa on my "beach cruiser"-bike. I take in the wooden houses painted in egg yellow and sea blue. They kind of remind me of those villages you see in westerns, with small veranda's, wooden shutters and ad signs with graceful lettering. Wait a minute. Is that a clothes rack with a sale on? For only one dollar?! I slow down and double back to the little store that is chock full of clothes racks.

"Aloha!" a woman with a voluminous curly bouffant greets me in a loud voice from behind the counter. "Go ahead and browse at your leisure. I won't be sticking to your back like a fly." But when I've tried on a white top with a plunging neckline and make a full turn in front of the mirror she does come over.

'Gorgeous!" she cries out. "That's just perfect for a party!"

Why oh why am I such a sucker for motivational words like these...

"I'll take it!"

"Pele!" I call out to the Fire Goddess. I'm standing outside again on the sunny pavement and feel extremely motivated to attract yet more pleasurable things. "I would like it to be a great evening, with a nice flirt to top it off." I recall Aunty's warning to clearly state your wishes. And so, just to be sure, I add: "And I'd like it to be a nice, sweet guy with a sense of humor. Oh yes, and a gorgeous body, please."

That afternoon I decide to go to a hypnotherapy workshop held in the lounge area of the Hawaiian Sanctuary. The topic was "The Power of Manifesting" and the hypnotist, Susan Bambara, worked in Hollywood, apparently even on a couple blockbusters including the Matrix Reloaded, someone whispered to me. She had decided to trade in the hectic film industry for a quiet life off-grid on the Big Island.

"It was my dream," Susan begins, "to help people find themselves again." I'm all ears when she tells us about the results she's achieved helping people use hypnosis to overcome their negative habits and difficult issues.

When she's finished, she asked if there were any questions and I raised my hand. "If I'm going to write a book, how can I manage to do it in one go, and is it possible to overcome writer's block with hypnosis?"

She moves her feet a bit further apart, places the tip of her elbows on her knees and folds her hands under her face. "There are easier ways to accomplish that. Make a habit of looking in the mirror every time you brush your teeth and to say to yourself: 'I am going to write a successful novel.' That way you're programming your brain to act upon it. Go ahead and try it out," she adds with a wink.

I secretly decide to practice with another sentence: "I'm going to meet a nice guy tonight."

The Hawaiian Sanctuary doesn't allow alcohol on the premises, but somehow people do manage to sneak in beer, vodka, whiskey and rum. A week ago I had my first taste of chocolate beer. Only after the last greedy gulp did I realize it contained alcohol. This was certainly no kiddy drink but the real thing and moreover, addictively delicious. I've popped a few cans into the fridge for tonight. The chocolate beer is meant as a backup for the cacao elixir they will be serving tonight. If that stuff turns out to be a disappointment, I can always fall back on my chocolate bubbles. However, judging from the raving reviews about the natural rush it's supposed to induce, I don't really expect I'll need to resort to that.

I look at my light pink lips, black eyelashes and sea-green fingernails. With the new top to top it off even I have to admit I look pretty stunning. It's been weeks since I felt this good and confident. I can already hear Andy in the distance, the deejay who lives on the property and who's now playing the first song of the evening.

"Bring it on!" I clap my hands with excitement and anticipation.

"Fancy a drink?" Bob asks me a little later. He's carrying two cacao elixirs and is positively beaming.

"Mahalo nui loa," I thank him in Hawaiian, downing it as

if it's a shot. The watery, somewhat bitter concoction vaguely reminds me of Dutch chocolate milk. An hour later I'm floating over the dance floor, analyzing the effects of the elixir. Like ecstasy, it induces a dream-like mood and feelings of love. It's a stimulant, like caffeine. And I absolutely love it. Still, halfway through the evening I find myself craving some of that dark gold liquid in the fridge. When I decide to go to get myself a can I discover I have a partner in crime. Will is a pretty solitary guy who goes about his duties during the day without mingling with the rest of us. But not tonight. We burst out laughing when we find out we both sneaked in here for the same reason.

Unfortunately the alcohol goes straight to my head and I end up making a terrible faux pas: I pour the beer into a glass but forget to leave it behind when I decide to return to the dance floor. And of all people there I end up bumping into the owner of the Hawaiian Sanctuary. She greets me with a friendly smile, until she sees the glass in my hand. "Is that beer?"

"Uh, yes," I stammer, "I believe it is." I quickly skedaddle out of sight. Outside, heart thumping inside my chest, I wonder if I will be asked to leave the property. "Oh heck, who cares?" I cry out boisterously and leg it back to the kitchen. Now that I've been caught in the act I might as well open the other cans and go back to my jungalow for a private little party of my own. All hyper with adrenalin I look up at the sky and shout: "And hey, what about that flirt that didn't show up. What a farce!"

When I walk on I hear a rustling sound behind me. Feral pigs! I quickly turn on my flashlight, point it at the spot where the sound seemed to be coming from and find myself face to face with a guy. I take a good look with my flashlight and see a pair of friendly eyes and a well-toned body leaning against the trunk of a tree. "Who are you? What are you doing here? And what are your plans?" I'm so rattled I bombard him with questions. He bursts out laughing. "I'm Liam and I'm trying to reach a friend who's not answering. And who are you?"

I take a swig of beer and give him the succinct version. "I live and work here. I just got caught with a beer and am now on my way to a private party in my jungalow. Do you want a sip or would you rather respect the alcohol-free zone?"

He leans forward and takes the can, meanwhile looking me over. "You're quite a sight with your blond hair and white top. Like an angel bearing beer. I'm actually kind of glad my friend didn't show up."

I propose grabbing another beer from the fridge and on our way to the kitchen we chat about the people at the party. Liam turns out to be a nice guy who moved here from the American mainland to study astronomy. And then I practically jump out of my skin because I feel something brushing past my leg.

"What was that?" I cry out.

"A cat," Liam remarks. I feel shivers down my spine. Here I am in the middle of the night with a guy I don't know and then suddenly there's a weird cat... It can't be a coincidence, can it? But then what is it? The feline keeps on jumping up at me with outstretched claws, so we decide to seek safety in my jungalow. Liam looks at me. I bet he wants to kiss me. But how old is this guy?! Twenty-three? I decide to ask him.

'Twenty-eight." He's still fixing me with his stare. "What a peculiar meeting. You. The cat."

He suddenly leans closer and resolutely kisses me on the lips. I immediately pull back. Am I ready for this? I really don't know. Liam senses I'm uncomfortable and puts his arm around me. That feels good, until my head decides to take charge again. Is it okay to be kissing someone so soon after Sander's passing away? And it's barely been three hours since I met him. What would Sander say? Can he see all of this?

We sit next to each other for a while, joking and chatting about my recent beer incident. Until he looks at me again and decides to give it another try. This time I ignore the thoughts in my head. We end up lying on my bed, kissing for hours, until my beautiful flirt vanishes into the dark night.

26 Bob Ganesh Marley

I stare at the green sponge in my hand, with thick globs of cacao stuck to it. No way am I going to be able to clean the rest of the dirty plates with this, and the murky water in the four washing-up bowls is not exactly helping either. The first bowl is meant for the 'rough' work. The next one is for soaking. The third is filled with cold water to rinse everything off, and the last one contains iodine to disinfect. One by one I lift up the heavy bowls and swiftly throw the dirty water on top of two purple passion fruit plants growing right outside the kitchen. I'd rather pour it down the sink, but Lewis' didactic words dissuade me. He's told me it's a waste of water and moreover, that the nutrients in the water are actually good for the plants.

I do get Lewis' and the Hawaiian Sanctuary's vision, but can't prevent a "sinful" thought from popping up: I really miss my dishwasher. And the next thing I know I find myself wondering what I'm doing here. I'm working non-stop and hardly have time to relax. Before and right after Sander's death it was a very good distraction, but I kind of think "it's high time for some quality time", to quote one of Sander's maxims yet again.

I pull off the rubber household gloves and walk to the wicker sofa to hatch a plan. What I'd really like is to rent a car and tour the island. Just thinking about it already gets me all excited. I want to meet the locals! I want to take in the natural beauty of this place! I want to be free!

A few hours later I'm driving on a narrow road that curves

around the black cliffs on the southern coast. And there are naupaka flowers absolutely everywhere. I glance at the empty seat next to me. Only nine months ago Sander was sitting there and we were enjoying the stunning Hawaiian scenery together. I feel a stab of pain and a wave of depressing thoughts threatens to drown out my temporary feeling of happiness. That's how quickly things can change; the vibrant splashes of color in the physical world are now illuminating all the dark, lonely places deep inside me. "Wake up, Li!" I rebuke myself. "You're living in your memories instead of seeing all the beautiful things around you right now!"

I turn the radio to a local station and hear a song that meant a lot to Sander and me: Major Lazor's "Be Free". The first time we heard it was at the Getty Museum in LA, where we and several hundred hip Californians ended up at a party to celebrate the end of a local summer festival.

I notice Sander gaping at all the suntanned bodies of women with itty-bitty tops that offer subtle views of colorful tattoos. He pinches my bum and puts his arm around me. "Hey, fashion chick," he cries out elated. "Why don't you use this for a small fashion report, or at least Tweet a couple of pictures? I'm pretty sure your followers would really dig this style." I follow his advice and take a couple of photos of striking outfits. I also take some of Sander, who feels seriously underdressed in his khaki-colored chinos and white V-necked shirt among all the dudes in skinny jeans, baseball caps and tattoos.

At some point we detach ourselves from the crowd and Sander pulls me close while we watch the flaming red fireball of the sun dip into the sea. And that's when we hear the song that would prove to be so important those last six months of his life. I knew what the lyrics meant to Sander and I knew what it was like to dream of a future that would never happen.

'Comin' down, feelin' like a battery hen
Waves won't break till the tide comes in
What will I do in the sunrise
What will I do without my dreams

I just can't believe
What they've done to me
We could never get free
I just wanna be
I just wanna dream'

I stop the car on the shoulder of the road. "No! San. I can't do this. I don't want to live on without you. Help!" Hysterically I start beating the steering wheel. When I've finally recovered after about thirty minutes I hear Bob Marley singing on the radio: *"I've got a message for you. I love you, I love you, I love you. And I want you to know right now."*

With bated breath I listen to the sentences that are repeated over and over, as if the song is stuck on repeat. This is Sander communicating with me through music again! I quickly sweep my bags off the passenger seat and whisper softly: "Would you please come and sit down next to me?"

Another half an hour later I stop at a grocery store in Hilo – the largest city on the island – where a small woman comes up to me. She introduces herself as Charlie. "Would you be able to give me a lift home? I don't live very far from here," she hesitantly asks.

"Of course. Get right in." During the drive we chat about her brother's six month old baby she's been looking after. "He and his girlfriend are no longer able to take care of Layla." She sounds very sad when she says that. "For me the little one is a blessing, because it means that although I'm 54, I can still be a mother."

She gives me directions to her house and takes out a twenty dollar-bill when we get there. "For the ride," she states. When I refuse she offers to put me up in her bed & breakfast. "If you ever need a place to stay, just give me a call, okay?" She insists on showing me the romantically furnished rooms with transparent flower curtains and comfy throws. I immediately feel at home in her dollhouse and ask for her card when she's finished her tour.

"You never know," I say with a wink, looking at the wall in front of me where I see pictures of Santana, Frank Zappa and Ziggy Marley.

Seeing Ziggy Marley suddenly reminds of something that happened thirteen years ago, when Sander and I were hitchhiking in Corsica, France.

On one of the last days of our vacation the roads are deserted. And no cars means no lift. In the scorching heat I traipse behind Sander who is trying to walk in the little bit of shade the wispy cork oaks provide. From the ravine next to us there's a pungent smell of decomposing dead cows that the local farmers dump there. We divide the last sips of water and stare into the distance. Sander takes a small tape recorder from my backpack and turns on our favorite Bob Marley-song: Everything is Gonna Be Alright. And what happens next is almost unbelievable. First a bus appears out of nowhere and takes us to the capital city of the island; past cliffs, mountain villages and vineyards. When we get off in Ajaccio we see a poster: Ziggy Marley is giving a free concert that very same evening. One of the songs he plays is "Everything is Gonna Be Alright".

I have the feeling my meeting Charlie was written in the stars, or that's what it seems like when later that same week I make up my mind to leave the Hawaiian Sanctuary. The freedom of that little road trip has wet my appetite. I'm craving for adventure. All it takes is one phone call to Charlie and I've got myself a new home. Aloha!

27   Charlie

'Akochang!" I yell out joyfully as soon as I spot my Japanese friend in the lounge. Akiko decided to pack her bags and quit her work at the Hawaiian Sanctuary a few weeks ago. She left at a moment's notice for the western coast of Big Island but has come back for a surprise visit precisely on my last day here. "Lichang!" She sounds just as elated when she responds by adding the same Japanese suffix "chang", which as I now know is a sign of friendship.

She looks surprised when she sees my backpack. "Hey, are you leaving as well?!"

"Yep, for the same reason you left. I want to relax a bit." I tell her about my extraordinary meeting and my new home.

"Do you think I could also stay there? I haven't found a good place to sleep yet."

"Of course!" My heart leaps up; I'm so happy to have one of my buddies back. I don't think this meeting today is a coincidence. Akiko provides me with the necessary comfort and sense of belonging and in return I am now able to give her a place to recover from the kidney infection she was suffering from a couple of months ago, which is the reason she's still not feeling fit. In fact, her body actually seems to have grown weaker.

Akiko has drawn the same conclusion as me. "The universe apparently wants us to take care of each other."

A few hours later Charlie welcomes us with green tea while we treat her to some chunks of raw Hawaiian Sanctuary chocolate we've brought with us.

She nibbles on it. "Oh my gosh. I have never ever tasted such pure chocolate. I'm going to have to take small bites of that, otherwise I'll turn completely hyper."

She later hands me an impressively thick surf magazine and tells us a bit more about her life. "Ten years ago I practically lived on my board. These days I hardly ever ride the waves; I've grown too old for that."

Dark clouds are gathering over the wooden house when I move to the cool room downstairs and plug in my laptop. The house is set on poles to protect it against floods. In 1940 a tsunami swallowed up part of the town and claimed hundreds of casualties, predominantly Japanese immigrants.

The cellar where I'm sitting is Charlie's massage area cum office space.

I like to come down here, and that's because of the internet connection. In this cubicle I can dissolve the thousands of miles between me and everything and everyone back home. Today I decide to contact Juuls via Skype. She's been in deep mourning since Sander's death and is one of my few girlfriends Sander also knew well, as they were college friends and had the same major.

"Saying goodbye to him made a huge impression on me." She sighs. "I wasn't sure if I should even go and see him. As the disease was progressing he'd clearly isolated himself and I didn't know if he'd even want me to sit there by his bed when he felt so incredibly vulnerable. He told me he 'understood'. And you know that at one point he was so bewildered he called me 'his little sister'. We both cracked up at that. I kissed him, I cuddled him and I whispered in his ear how much you love him. He was incredibly happy to hear that. It really seemed to calm him."

And then she tells me she wants to say something about the mail she sent earlier, asking me if I was certain I wanted to stay on Big Island. "I now realize you really gave it a lot of thought about what felt best for you. And I understand that because you'd already been through such an ordeal that you couldn't face another one of those battles on top of an extremely difficult flight back to Holland. But I am glad I voiced my doubts, as it forced you to reconsider your decision and helped you determine this really was the only way. It was kind of like a double check. But it must have been so difficult for you, Li."

"Yeah, you're right about that. But it's okay now, Juuls. Really."

She tells me a bit more about what the impact of saying goodbye to Sander had on her, and that emotionally she was so drained she filled her days with work, work, and yet more work.

In an attempt to wash off the call I decide to take a dip in the salty seawater. That helps, a little bit. When I'm sitting on the beach after my swim my thoughts invariably go back to Sander. I miss the stable, protective factor he was in my life and imagine myself leaning on his strong shoulder. He puts his arm around me. And we stay like that for a good long while, our heads close together.

I ask him to give me a sign he's with me now. In less than sixty seconds a dolphin suddenly jumps out of the water, twirls in the air and disappears again. I blink. Did that really just happen?

The next morning I decide to put on my running shoes hoping to spot some more dolphins in the bay of Hilo. Running is one of the ways I'm attempting to ground myself because this island sometimes seems to go straight to my head. That dolphin yesterday for instance; it seemed so real. Or was it my imagination after all? I run along the calm waterline and see the first fishing boats leaving to catch fresh ahi, with which Hawaiians make a delicious dish called poke. On the street I see burst mango fruit and birds that are treating themselves to the sweet snack. I pass bushes and trees with avocado, passion fruit and noni fruit. With their white jelly and prickly skin the latter look almost otherworldly. Underneath a tree with leaves in the shape of rosettes I see a Japanese man silently enjoying the view. I slow down to greet him. We chat a bit about his grandchildren and the sea turtles who now and then stick their heads out of the water.

"Do you know if there are dolphins here as well?"

He shakes his head. "I sit here every morning, but I've never yet seen one."

See, I think, disappointed, it can't have been a dolphin then.

The man suddenly pats my arm, all excited and with a distinct sparkle in his eyes. "But look what I found on the beach this morning." He points towards the exact spot where I was sitting last night and puts his hand in his pocket. On the palm of his hand I see a shiny little figurine of a dolphin

28 Cosmic coiffeur

After one and a half months of slogging away on the Hawaiian Sanctuary my inch-long dark roots are making me feel like a slob and I decide to treat myself to a nice new blond haircut. Time to turn the hippie lady back into a hip lady! When I walk into a modern-looking beauty parlor in one of Hilo's smarter neighborhoods I automatically recall a very special encounter in a hair salon in downtown Utrecht that turned out to be a life-changing experience.

I'm curled up in bed with a splitting headache, ice-cold feet and a tear-soaked pillow. Last night Sander broke his promise once again; I found him with a liter of vodka under his belt.

Why does life have to be so incredibly difficult? Is this what my life is going to be like from now on? I've been missing my buddy for quite some time now. I hate his alter ego that's drowning in fear and vodka. Should I break up with him and leave? If only Sander were here with me now, if only he would comfort me. I roll onto my back and try to let go of my worries while relaxing my cramped muscles and angrily shout towards the ceiling, to God, to the angels, or to the universe itself: "Help me in a way that really helps me! I see green colors, but what good is that?! Talk to me!"

In an attempt to break through these emotions I decide to treat myself to a new haircut; a good reason to get out of the house as well. A few hours later I open the door of the chic hair salon "Rob Peetoom" in the center of town, completely covered in snowflakes. A friendly-looking guy gives me the once-over, shakes his head and takes my coat. "Girl, you'd better get yourself warmed up first."

After a cup of tea and a hair dying session that takes several hours, I see him again after my hair has been rinsed and washed.

"Just lie down and relax now," he says, and begins massaging my head. The splitting headache disappears like snow in summer. And something else happens as well, something pretty peculiar. As soon as I close my eyes I see intense green and purple colors merging together. Wanting to check if he's aware of this, I remark: "You seem to have healing hands; my headache is gone!"

He introduces himself as Matthijs and tells me he's a clairsentient. "I sometimes pick up things from people. For instance I just happen to know you're a joyful, energetic woman who would do anything for her friends but that you tend to eliminate yourself from the equation." He pauses and goes on. "I also see you're not good at choosing and find it difficult to make decisions. This morning you weren't sure if you should stay home or leave. But deep in your heart you already know the answer."

I gasp.

"You're going through a really difficult time, right?"

I look at Matthijs and grab his arm. "Are you real or are you an angel?"

He laughs. "Right now you could use a little external help. That's what I sense and that's why I'm telling you this."

I want to tell him he's right, that I wanted to leave Sander this morning, but that he's very sick and...

"You don't have to tell me," he interrupts my thoughts. "I know. I know your boyfriend is very ill. I know what

you're going through. This morning and last night were very difficult, right? You should know that you boyfriend is terribly afraid. It's paralyzing him. He feels lonely and doesn't know what to do."

I ask him if he knows what the future will bring but he's not allowed to disclose that. "It's important that he listens to his body and takes better care of it," Matthijs says. "Nothing is set in stone," he continues. "But remember that when things get to be too heavy at home, it's good to go outside. You could try to break through the situation by getting some fresh air at the beach. Tell him you love him. Take him by the hand and let him follow you."

I struggle to understand what he's saying, trying to put two and two together. Matthijs senses that. "Just let it go. Don't think about it. You don't need to." He places his hands on my head. "And now we're going to lower your heart rate." I immediately relax and even feel a small glimmer of happiness and hope.

We exchange contact details and hug each other. A few weeks after meeting Matthijs, I come to the conclusion that I can no longer stay with Sander and have to save myself from this impossible situation. We decide to break up.

"Aloha! Highlights, please," I greet the hairdresser in the mirror. I've confidently installed myself in the chair where I expect to stay for the next couple of hours. Within fifteen minutes my head is covered with a thick layer of tinfoil and the hairdresser has more or less filled me in on her life story. She grew up in San Francisco, moved to Big Island with her parents, met the man of her dreams and is now pregnant with their second child; a girl.

"She'll be here in a few weeks." She lovingly strokes her

stomach.

"Do you already know her name? Oops, I'm really sorry. Maybe you don't want to tell me. I sometimes am a bit too direct."

She laughs. "Don't worry, that's fine. I'd be glad to share it with you. We're going to call her Halia, in memory of my grandmother. In Hawaiian that name means 'memory of a dear departed loved one'."

I straighten up in shock. It's a Hawaiian tradition to give people a specific Hawaiian name next to their "normal" name. That is, if you're lucky; but how, what and when you receive that name is up to the universe. I know Anna, the Australian lady at the Hawaiian Sanctuary, got the same name as Charlie's little girl: Layla.

"Halia" happens to be my name as well and the meaning of the word is so apt. The name is in honor of Sander and my father but also symbolizes a new start for myself. As I'll be sitting under the dryer for some thirty minutes or so I decide to write a short account of this special encounter on my travel blog. Sander and I started that blog nine months ago to keep the home front informed about our trip to the US and Kaua'i. It was during that trip that I discovered that the name "Halia" also has the name "Li" in it, which is short for "Lideweij". Just like Hawaii also has a "ha" in it.

I raise my head to look in the mirror in front of me. What?! *Do I see a completely white head there?* Oh no! She's dyed everything a high-lift blond instead of just giving me highlights. I bet it looks totally ridiculous! Oh no! W*ait a minute...* Last night I was actually considering dying all my hair because I know it makes you look younger and "fresher". Have I perhaps unconsciously manifested this result?

And then I suddenly hear Sander's voice. "Lookin' good Li, but maybe you should reassure that poor girl." He gestures and only then I notice the hairdresser's face has turned stark-white.

"Sorry about that," I say. "I'm actually really glad you did this. You've made me very happy today. The 'old me' returned in the wake of my new blond hair."

She sighs with relief and meticulously blow-dries my white hydrogen peroxide locks.

When I arrive back at Charlie's place she's looking fabulous in a straw hat and cream-colored transparent top. Deep inside she's still a young girl who would rather go out every evening, but because of the baby she can no longer do that.

I ask Charlie what she thinks about my hair. "A blonde! My my, you'll be very popular with the men around here," she says with a wink. "Girl, you look gorgeous! Wait, I've got just the thing for your new look." She takes me by the hand to the closet in her bedroom. "Here! This will look absolutely perfect on you." She takes a yellow and pink halter dress from a hanger and holds it out in front of me. "That's beautiful," she mutters. "Too bad it's about five sizes too large." She dives back into the closet and comes out with a gown to die for. It's cream-colored, with a tight-fitting embroidered bodice. A super sexy dress! "Chop chop, go and try it on," she instructs me.

When I try it on in my own room and catch sight of myself in the mirror I immediately think of the wedding gown I once tried on in a bridal boutique in Zutphen, a town in the eastern part of The Netherlands.

My mother and sisters-in-law urge me to try on the dream dress that just happens to be hanging in the shop window. Sander and I got engaged last month. Although a vague feeling tells me there's never going to be a wedding, I'm like a little girl in a candy store when I point to the highlight of the collection. The dress is off-white, with a strapless bodice and a wide band of frilly tulle at the hem. The saleslady chuckles at my very resolute choice and escorts me to a large fitting room where she helps me to put it on, which is no easy feat.

When I turn around and look in the mirror my hands automatically go to my lips. "Oh! It's gorgeous." As soon as I've left the fitting room and my mother and my sisters-in-law see me, they react the exact same way.

"That's your dress," Mariël, the wife of my eldest brother, whoops.

"That dress was made for you," adds Irene, my youngest brother's girlfriend. I make a full turn in front of the mirror, stand on my tippy toes and make a deep curtsey for my own reflection which I will never again see like it is now.

And now it's Charlie who puts her hand to her lips. "Absolutely stunning! Now all we need is a bridegroom." I take in my suntanned body that has become a lot leaner and more toned due to the yoga classes, the jogging, the workouts and all the physical labor at the Hawaiian Sanctuary. But Charlie has magically transformed me from a tough looking farmer girl into a ravishing princess. "I'd like to give you that," she says, "as a present."

"Are you serious?" I look at her in the mirror. "But I can't possibly accept this." But she won't take no for an answer so I quickly throw my arms around her neck. Later that afternoon we pop open a couple of cans of beer and toast to today while I silently thank all the extraordinary people who've crossed my path here. And I also drink to Halia, the woman who has rediscovered herself and is radiant, internally as well as externally.

You're not alone
even though you might not notice that.
No need to be afraid,
there's always an arm around your shoulder.

Let life be easy
all you need to do is ask

And take a look at yourself.
Not only at the external you,
but feel on the inside as well,
and cherish both.

Halia

29 Westside

My tummy is rumbling. I've still got one bar of raw chocolate with dates in my room. I eagerly sink my teeth into it and walk outside where Charlie is having coffee with a friend; a stocky guy with a baseball cap who's slightly cross-eyed. I shake his hand and introduce myself.

"Lide," Charlie cries out. "This is my friend Earl. Weren't you looking for a *Kahuna,* a medicine woman? Well, you've found one." She starts laughing. I look from her to Earl and back to her with question marks in my eyes.

"He's a Kahu, the male version of a Kahuna, in other words: a teacher or a priest," she explains.

"You can call me Ku," Earl says, throwing me a smile from under his cap.

"Are you serious?" I look at my housemate again, still not quite believing it. "Well, then I guess I *am* looking for you!" I cry out elated. "I mean, I was looking for a Kahuna, but I don't mind a male shaman."

And before I know it I've invited myself over to Ku's place. He lives at an hour's drive from Hilo, near Ka Lae, towards the southernmost tip of the island.

"You're more than welcome to stop by," Earl answers. "And I can tell you everything you want to know about the Fire Goddess Pele. You will actually pass her Halema'uma'u Crater on the way to my place."

I decide to combine my visit to Ku's by moving on to a different accommodation as well; to the Manago Hotel in Captain Cook. It's a delightful place on one of the best locations of the island: crystal-clear water, tropical fish *and* spinner dolphins. Besides Ku the latter is one of the main reasons I decide to leave for the western coast.

I drag myself to the kitchen where Charlie is feeding Layla little bites of apple pancake. Just seeing the greasy dough already makes my mouth water but I'm still on my diet of no wheat, no sugar and no butter. When Layla throws me a big smile I melt just as easily as the dab of butter in Charlie's sizzling frying pan. Gosh, I'm really going to miss these two.

We exchange big hugs and presents. I give Charlie a picture of a shooting star. She gives me the gorgeous dress but we both feel this is not a final goodbye. Something tells me I'll come back here. Layla smiles at me and tries to imitate Donald Duck; a sound I used to attract her attention only a week ago.

I start the engine of the rental car and leave Charlie's premises to move on to Earl's house in Pahala. According to my sat nav – the only modern gadget on board – I will be arriving in 1 hour and 11 minutes at precisely 1.01 pm.

Driving on Highway 101 I think of Sander again. "That's seven times one, San!" I cry out cheerfully. "That means the angels are with me!"

I soon leave the city behind me and have to clear my ears a few times because of the change in altitude. Underneath this road there's fire-hot magma: I'm getting close to Fire Goddess' Pele's home. The local radio station plays a Phil Collins song; a musician my father used to like to listen to on the *Route du Soleil* when we'd go to French Riviera for our family's summer vacation. My men are with me, I know that. Sander and my dad are in the back sharing a chocolate beer.

During the drive to the other side of the island I let my

mind wander freely. How is it that I've left everything behind and gone to Hawaii? Which answers am I hoping to find here?

"We will help you find all the answers," Phil Collins tells me via the speakers in the car. Wow! Did that really happen? I'm almost getting used to things like this occurring just like that.

I enter National Volcano Park, a landscape of endless black rocks, and drive past the Fire Goddess' crater. I've decided I will bring her an offering of flowers and red wine on the way back.

Once I take the exit off the highway I find myself on a steep road lined with modern row homes. Within a few minutes I've arrived at Ku's house, which is surrounded by Green Ti, a plant which according to ancient Hawaiian wisdom possesses protective powers. I've been told it's a good idea to pick a leaf before you hit the road, so naturally I did that this morning. Ku is waiting for me in the garden and chuckles when he sees the green leaf on the dashboard.

"Smart thing to do before you set off. It means you were well-protected during your trip," he says, giving me an aloha-hug. I have to admit he looks pretty cool for a shaman, with his baseball cap, olive-green shirt and brown pants with cargo pockets.

Ku picks a Green Ti leaf and begins to talk. "I'm a bit like this plant, a protector of the region and its inhabitants. That's what my name 'Ku' actually means." He rolls up the sleeve of his right arm and shows me the face of a warrior, a tattoo made with very fine lines and pointy little triangles. "I had this done by a Maori man in New Zealand, a very spiritual man. He sensed that I would fulfill a very important mission in this world and wanted to express that. It took him hours to do this. I wasn't allowed to move while he was in deep meditation and his ancestors told him what the tattoo was supposed to look like." He rolls down his sleeve again.

"We're one big family, an *ohana*. You're also part of that.

You were in Hawaii in a former life and your ancestors have called you back here." He cocks his head and raises it slightly, just like Aunty did a few weeks ago, as if to channel a message from the universe. "They're telling me I should perform a healing ritual with you on the holy mountain and I think I'd better listen to them." He chuckles. "Would you like that?"

We drive through a very Hawaiian looking community, passing a group of cute-looking girls in school uniforms of black pleated skirts and polo shirts. The influence of the US mainland is less visible in this remote corner, not like in the larger towns, where there's tons of new and well-known American hotel chains, resorts and supermarkets, like Safeway and Walmart.

Ku slows down and rolls down his window. "Aloha, Bill!" he shouts to the only white man on the street. When I'm introduced to him he tells me in his thick Southern drawl: "Thanks to Ku's fight against real estate developers, nature here on the southern coast has fortunately remained unspoiled. You won't find any resorts around here." The two men say goodbye with the typical Hawaiian balled fist and pinky gesture.

We drive on past fields of macadamia trees aligned in perfectly neat rows. The car engine is having trouble with the steep hill, while I take in the lush green meadows with grazing horses and cows. In the distance I see a mountain that reminds me of the South African Table Mountain: a very broad base with a flat top.

"We call this area Kumaua, home of the Rain God Kaiholena. He used to be a man of flesh and blood who wanted to start a banana plantation. He asked Pele for permission to work her soil. She agreed under one condition: that he would give her his first harvest. However, Kaiholena forgot their deal and the furious goddess turned him into a mountain; white on the bottom, black at the top." Ku switches to a lower gear and continues with his story. "When Hawaii was colonized by the Americans, a certain 'Mr. Surf' wanted to develop the mountain. He blew up part of the land without paying due respect to the Rain God. It led to a terrible downpour and the house of the pig-headed man was swept away. Mr. Surf himself went missing for days until one of the villagers found his body on the banks of a river, half-eaten by feral pigs." Ku turns to me with a piercing look: "Legends are still very much alive and kicking here, don't ever forget that!"

In front of us an immense plain with fluorescent green grass and trees and bright red flowers appears, with the enormous bluish gray expanse of the ocean behind it. I see bright yellow butterflies as big as my hand glide by my car window. I feel so insignificant in the face of this magnificent natural beauty.

Ku parks by the side of the road. "This is a good spot for a healing." He opens the trunk and takes out a white and pink sea shell. "I'm going to blow on this three times to invite ancestors; the four natural elements of water, fire, earth and air, and the four directions of the wind to take part in the ritual. The only thing you have to do is find yourself a quiet spot and relax."

I decide to go and stand in a sort of opening among high grass stalks with a good view of the immense ocean in front of me. I close my eyes while Ku blows his shell and starts singing an old Hawaiian chant. It's almost as if I know the words of the prayer and when I softly hum along, I feel my body starting to rock back and forth. I quickly open my eyes and look around me. *Who is doing this?* Ku is several feet away from me. Could it be the wind? I inhale and exhale deeply, trying to stop the thoughts in my head. Shortly afterward I feel the same thing again, as if the island itself is bobbing on the waves of the ocean. The motion becomes more and more pronounced until I almost lose my balance. The powers Ku is invoking cannot be seen with the naked eye but are certainly felt.

He later confirms that. "Not everyone is able to deal with this kind of energy. For some people it's too intense. Some even start levitating." He takes my hand and pats it gently. "You had to come here, you know. Not only for this ritual. I've also received a message."

"A message?"

He nods. "Yes, you will find what you seek. You will find yourself."

Back in the car Ku tells me about his long journey before becoming a shaman. "My wife had died and I felt terribly lonely. It was an awfully difficult period. I retreated to a little house by the ocean, where the sea and years of meditation helped me come to terms with my grief, until I was finally able to let it go. Isolated and amidst the silence of nature I also discovered I had a mission: I had to become a Kahu. It was only afterward that I realized my wife's death was a sort of awakening for me. She was a spiritual woman, who knew everything there is to know about Hawaiian rituals and traditions. From the other side she is assisting me to become a Ku."

His story is mesmerizing and punctuated with wise lessons. "Modesty is an important quality for inner evolution. Or, like the Dalai Lama says: *One finds oneself by dissolving the ego.* Lots of people primarily value materialistic things. They want an even bigger car, or an expensive vacation or a second home. But the only thing that ends up growing is the emptiness inside themselves and they continue to feel the lack. The energy on Earth is getting more and more powerful. Now is a good time to state your wishes and dreams. But be careful, Halia, be very clear about what you want because you might just get what you ask for."

Ku is the first one to call me by my new name; it suddenly

sounds so official. When I hug him a few minutes later and want to say goodbye, he shakes his head in refusal. "No, we Hawaiians don't say goodbye. Goodbye doesn't exist. We will see each other again, wherever that may be. And you are going to come back to Big Island," he says. His eyes become larger. "You're going to cure someone together with me."

On my way back to the hotel I say "mahalo" out loud, grateful for this beautiful day. Ever since I re-found my inner peace and sense of freedom, life has been showering me with wise lessons and confronting me with teachers at moments I least expect it. Only a month ago I thought I had to seek all the answers within myself but now I know there's always help out there, be it from a shaman or a hairdresser in a suburb. I now greet each day with curiosity and without any expectation, totally different from what my life was like only six months ago. Expectations block the flow and the natural flow of life. Hawaiians believe in courage and confidence when letting go of expectations, knowing there's always something more beautiful on the horizon.

30 Dolphins

For over a week now I've faithfully been getting up at seven o'clock every morning to walk to a little bay. I've heard this is the place where spinner dolphins come to rest after their nocturnal forage. And because I desperately want to meet them I've been sitting here for days, on my little beach mat, staring out over the surface of the water. Once, in the far distance, I saw them jump out of the water. I set off in pursuit of them via a winding coastal path that led me to one of the most beautiful underwater worlds of Big island: Honaunau Bay. I even went swimming with the *Honu,* the big sea turtles that are considered to be a good luck charm by Hawaiians but unfortunately, the dolphins didn't show up.

But on the very last day of my stay on the western coast I finally spot them. I race to the water's edge, swimming like a total madwoman towards the spot where I saw them. In the distance I see the first spinner dolphin jump out of the water. Because it's quite windy the waves are choppy and are trying to push me back to shore. Determined and with powerful strokes – which unfortunately also means swallowing several gulps of seawater – I finally manage to reach the magical water creatures. Underwater I see a fanatic diver imitating their swimming strokes by making kicking motions with her legs but she's actually chasing them away. Disappointed I see their shiny bodies leave the bay.

I start on the long swim back towards the beach and suddenly recall Madonna's song "The Power of Goodbye". That was the song I heard on the radio right before saying goodbye to Sander. I sing the first sentence out loud: "Your heart is not open..."

And then... Wow! Choking on more seawater I see tens of fins heading in my direction! Did I attract them with my singing? I start humming the song a bit louder and within a few seconds they've formed a blue-gray circle around me. A baby dolphin shoots past me, twirling playfully in the air, only to dive back into the water in a beautiful perfect straight line.

"Amazing!" I yell excitedly, and even clap. "This is unbelievable! I can't believe this is really happening!"

The dolphins are making me laugh and that's exactly what I had hoped they would do. They're waking up my inner child. This was one of the reasons why I really wanted to encounter them. They bring back a sense of joy and spontaneity that I'd lost during those incredibly tough and long years of Sander's disease. I now know why dolphins are also called "angels of the sea". They also invoke a feeling of safety and trust, but most of all of joy and happiness. I will never forget this encounter.

"Aloha!" I hear someone say behind me. I wasn't expecting anyone. I quickly turn around and see a small, slender woman in her mid-forties looking at me. Wait a minute, I know who that is! It's the Italian woman, Shola, one of the meditation teachers from the Hawaiian Sanctuary. I was going to do a so-called "soul hunt" with her - an old Indian ritual where you go in search of the big questions of life - but we never ever actually managed to set a date. And here she is now, just like that, on a secluded beach on the other side of the island.

"This can't be a coincidence," she concludes. "Your soul hunt is meant to be." I nod affirmatively but also feel a bit bewildered due to all these extraordinary meetings.

"Are you free tomorrow?" I ask. "That's my very last day on the island." After we've agreed on a time and location she takes my hand, looking at me clear-eyed, and says: "It's going to be very special. I'm looking forward to it."

31   Visiting Pele

*"Logic will get you from A to B,
imagination will take you everywhere."*

Albert Einstein

Darn. Once again I wake up very early; getting eight hours of
sleep apparently just isn't going to happen anymore. Is this
healthy or just plain fatiguing? I haven't figured it out yet but
I don't actually feel that tired. Here, on the western coast of
Big Island, I only get five, six hours of sleep at night, at most.
The sun is still hiding behind the tall mountain but the roosters
in the garden of the hotel are already screaming their heads
off. I pull the Hawaiian flowery throw over my head and try
to get some more sleep. And then all of a sudden my whole
bed starts shaking. An earthquake! Exactly one minute before
my alarm-clock is about to go off. Could that be Pele making
sure I don't oversleep? Today is the day of my return to the
east coast; to Charlie and Layla, in Hilo.

On the way back I want to make a stop on the mountain
where Ku took me as well as visit the Fire Goddess' crater.
The earthquake is over. I say a quick prayer, asking the spirits
of the island to protect me.

Standing in the parking lot I look out over the immense
ocean in front of me. The sky is a light orange. The first rays
of sunlight have arrived. I pick up a frangipani flower lying

at my feet and take in the sweet smell. *Oh, how I'm going to miss this Hawaiian nature...* I start the old Nissan Sedan and head for the main road, slightly reluctantly taking leave of the rocky small bay I can still spot from the coastal road I'm driving on. The tarmac is half-covered with mangoes and red-colored birds are picking at the sweet pulp. *Hey, that would be a lovely breakfast.* After a short stop the back seat of the car is covered with fruit.

After one and a half hours I'm back on the rugged southern coast of Hawaii, with huge waves crashing against the black cliffs. The first time I saw this I didn't particularly like it. It was Ku who showed me the hidden beauty in the dark-brown rocks, pointing out there were also light pink and fluorescent green hues. When I arrive at the spot where Ku performed the healing ritual, I stop the car and thank the spirits. "Mahalo!" I shout towards the mountain, taking a deep bow. I take a blue stone out of my pocket and place it on the rock. "This is for you, to thank you for the healing." I end by singing an old Hawaiian prayer and stand there listening to the rustling leaves of the trees in the wind.

And then I recall Ku's words: "You have to go and see the Fire Goddess. She wants you to come by." I pick a few branches with bright yellow flowers, get back in the car, put the key in the ignition and drive on to Volcano National Park, Pele's home base. After a drive of almost two hours I see the first billowing plumes of smoke. When I've parked by the side of the crater I follow the directions to a viewing area; Ku was kind enough to write down the exact coordinates for me. Few tourists venture here, so I can bring my offering in all peace and quiet. I crawl underneath a fence to be able to get even closer to the crater's edge. Thick smoke rises up towards the sky.

"Pele!" I shout to the vast and rugged lunar landscape. "It's me, Halia. I've brought you something."

The pungent smell of alcohol hits me when I pour half a bottle of red wine on the black soil. I take a big gulp myself and toast to the Fire Goddess. "Mahalo, Pele, for bringing me to Big Island. I don't believe you tried to pull Sander and me apart like you did with the two lovers in the legend of Naupaka. To the contrary, I think you are trying to reunite us. Can you give me a sign whether that's true?"

I watch the crater closely. Is that bubbling lava I see? Do I hear hissing gas? No, nothing. When I close my eyes again and thank Pele a second time I feel her fiery power stir in my abdomen. All at once I see a woman in front of me; a woman with a square face and piercing eyes. Could that be Pele? She puts her index finger against her lips. "Hulu," she says, and at the same time a swirling flow of lava appears behind her. The red orange mass flows through the earth, twisting and turning, and ends up forming the figure eight. That's the infinity sign!

For me it symbolizes the infinite love between Sander and me. When the image has disappeared I take out my iPhone and quickly look up the word Pele whispered to me. Google tells me Hulu "is the Hawaiian word for feather, a sign that the boundary between the physical and the spiritual world is an illusion."

I kneel down to kiss the ground full of wonder, feeling intensely grateful.

And then I walk back to the car to drive on to my next adventure: my soul hunt with Shola.

32   Soul hunt

Shola's garden is the perfect rendering of the Biblical Garden of Eden where Adam and Eve lived. I see big bunches of red hibiscus flowers, green palm leaves, lilac-colored orchids and magnificent views of the crystal-clear ocean. The jungalow where she lives, works and sleeps seems to glow in the magical golden afternoon sun. The Italian woman has chosen one of the prime spots in Puna, on the southeastern coast of Big Island, where the purest air anywhere on earth has been recorded.

"Lide!" she cries out excitedly, hugging me tightly as soon as I walk into the garden. "I'm so happy you're going to do this soul hunt with me." She welcomes me into her little house that has four walls of sturdy green gauze, just like my jungalow at the Hawaiian Sanctuary. On an oak desk there's a canvas of a bright yellow frangipani flower, with two missing petals.

"It's the perfect spot for painting," says Shola, pointing towards the sun with a smile. "Even better than the light in Tuscany."

In a modern little kitchen with a grey-blue stone counter Shola prepares us tea with fresh herbs from her garden. I lean down to take in the smell of rosemary and thyme that rises up from the big pan on the stove.

"Is this your first soul hunt ever?" she asks. I nod. Shola takes a sip of her herbal tea. "As the name indicates you will be going in search of a part of your lost soul. I gather you've already given it some thought. What is it going to be about?"

Yes, I'm quite certain this is going to be about my self-confidence, which has taken a terrible knock after Sander's "change of address". Our lives were as close as two intertwined tree trunks and now that we can no longer lean on each other my own trunk has to become strong enough to hold me upright.

"I'm going to put you into a deep trance through rapid breathing while beating on a shaman drum," she explains. "And then I will blindfold you to prevent your surroundings from distracting you."

I immediately feel shivers down my spine; a blindfold means I have to surrender myself completely. Shola notices my unease and reassures me. "Don't worry. If anything should happen we will immediately take it off. Go ahead and lie down on the floor."

I take off my slippers and lie down. My heart is beating so fast you can see the thin blanket Shola has placed on top of me moving slightly.

"Okay, now just follow me." She starts breathing in quick, short gasps. Due to the extra oxygen in my brain it only takes me a few minutes to start feeling a bit woozy and light in the head. My thoughts come to a standstill; Shola leans forward and blindfolds me with a black cloth. "Relax and think about the part of yourself you want to heal. Don't resist, just let it come over you."

"Self-confidence, self-confidence, self-confidence," I repeat over and over like a mantra in eager anticipation of what will happen next. Nothing. I let Shola's rhythmic beating on the drum sweep over me and feel myself sinking into a deep trance.

I find myself walking over a black lava plain and recognize the area of the hike that night Bob took us to see the lava stream. When I glance to my right I see the Fire Goddess is leading me by the hand. She's beautiful, with eyes as dark as solidified lava and her long hair looks as if it's braided with red-orange flames.

Pele jumps into a churning lava stream, pulling me with her. Without burning I slip into the sticky orange-colored syrup, entering subterranean caves and ending up in the bedroom of my apartment back in The Netherlands. The time is six months ago and I'm huddled against the white chest of drawers. My body is contorted with spasms of sorrow. Sander has drunk himself into a delirium and has totally lost it. I feel terribly let down and am staring at the floor in despair. Pele appears in front of me with blazing eyes. "Burn it all!"

I get up and pull the drawers out of the chest in a frenzy, stomping on the wood to make it into kindling. In no time the whole room is aflame. Despair, sorrow and loneliness: those are the emotions that travel through my body like electric shock waves, flowing out of my mouth where they ignite into flames. Pele puts a consoling arm around my shoulder and pulls me close. Her touch stirs up feelings of love. And lust. I reach out to stroke her soft cheek and neck. My hand moves to her round breasts and her hips. She reacts with soft kisses and then suddenly blows warm air into my ear. I pull back. From a distance I perceive how her hands turn into the claws of a cat. She makes scratching movements and starts to howl with laughter. And then it hits me, suddenly it's all clear. That cat that jumped up on me that one night was the Fire Goddess; she was warning me: no men for now, now is the time for self-love.

She again pulls me close and caresses my head. I hang in her arms, paralyzed like prey, surrendering myself to her completely. She presses her lips to mine firmly, kisses my neck softly, but then suddenly starts biting and gobbling up my flesh. She straightens up, takes a deep breath and roars in victory like a lioness. No. Wait. This is our victory! Because the Fire Goddess and I are one.

"Halia!" A woman with long silver-grey hair is calling me. She's sitting on a rock formation with a view of the ocean and spreads her arms as if she wants to embrace the water. The look in her eyes is one of intense happiness and self-confidence. That's me at the end of my life! I lie down on the warm sun-soaked rocks and surrender myself to the other world with complete trust. Via a tunnel of transparent fish I'm transported to a place where Sander and my father are waiting for me. I run up to them and leap into Sander's arms. We cry and kiss full of happiness. Although it already seems like he departed a long time ago, our love is as strong as ever. He takes my face in his hands and speaks to me in a soft voice: "Dear Li, we have to let each other go." I grab his waist with both hands in protest.

"Listen, sweetheart. You're not really dead yet. You still have a life to live on Earth. And you can determine your own path."

When I want to walk back to the path I've just come from, Sander stops me. "Hey, hold your horses. Look to your right." He points towards a road that looks like it's just been paved. "Ah, of course! You mean I have to take the new road," I deduce, kissing him on the cheek. When I place my foot on the new road Sander gives me an encouraging pinch in my bum. "I always keep my promises!" he laughs.

A soft bell brings me back to Shola's jungalow. I'm surprised that although I'm still blindfolded I can see everything in the room. And there's someone standing next to me. That is to say, I see a pair of long legs. The body connected to it towers high above the jungalow. This is no man of flesh and blood. That much is clear.

"Thank you for the stone and the ancient chant," the friendly voice of an old man tells me. "You couldn't see me but I was there."

Is this one of the spirits from the holy place Ku took me to? The man takes my hand and in a flash we're standing on the mountain on the south coast of Big Island with a view of the rough sea. "I not only protect this mountain," he begins, "but also the last bit of unspoiled nature on the island." He points at the sky where I see thousands of twinkling stars although it's bright daylight. "And that's where I come from."

"Will you please show me your world?" I'm staring at his legs that go way up into the clouds – they are the reason I'm still unable to see his face.

"One day I certainly will," he replies. "But now is not the time. You have to complete another journey first, and for now that's enough. You will return to this place on Big Island and learn more about Hawaiian healing rituals. And one day we will meet again." He takes out the blue stone I left on the mountain and crushes it with his fingers. "As of now I'm your protector," he says with a mysterious smile on his lips. "I have to go now. The shaman will blow light into your heart."

The spirit disappears and Shola places her hands on my breast. She blows briefly and forcefully into the small circle of her hands. And then my father shows up, with his familiar loving smile. He takes my hand to take me back in time, sixteen years to be exact, to that day he suffered a cardiac arrest and ended up in hospital in critical condition. Before my father had been a strong and caring man. After that he became a very fearful and insecure person. I'm sitting on his bed; crying, and feeling very scared. I'm afraid of losing him. He sits down next to me, puts his arm around me and rocks me gently to comfort me. And then it's my turn to take him by the hand to return to the place where he had his cardiac arrest, right in front of the town hall of Rheden, a town in the Dutch province of Gelderland. From a distance we regard the whole scene: how he gets off his bike to the moment his heart gives out. Only nothing happens. No, he gets back on his bike, cycles home whistling, eats his dinner of kale with mashed potatoes, gets into bed and wakes up with the alarm clock instead of the alarm of the intensive care.

His heart is beating.
His heart is alive.
He is living his heart.

We've both been healed.

It's all quiet and dark. Is this the end of the soul hunt? No, because I hear Shola beating the drum again. I decide to call Sander, because there's something only he can help me with.

"San, a year ago you told me something I haven't been able to forget. We were in the kitchen together when you suddenly said that when you were no longer there I should get together with a friend of ours. I wasn't able to react to it then because I was so shocked by what you'd just said. I didn't want to hear it and didn't want to face the fact that I might lose you. But I can't help but wonder why you said that."

Sander appears in front of me with a frown on his forehead. "Do you really want to know?"

"Yes!"

"Then why don't you go ahead and explore that," he says with a wink, only to disappear again.

What a weird reaction... Why should I go and explore that? And more importantly: how? Beseeching the sky with my hands I call out to the universe: "Please show me what this man means." I find myself on a beach where I see him, Steef, in the distance. I run up to him and greet him. No reaction. He's staring at the ground, unaware of his surroundings. I walk around him with a strange, indefinable feeling. It's like he's dazed. I tickle his side and gently nudge his shoulder. That works because he lifts his head a tiny bit and looks at me with empty eyes. Only he still doesn't see me. "Steef!" I yell, shaking his shoulder vigorously. "Wake up! What's wrong with you?"

At last he turns to me with a look of recognition, followed by a broad smile. "Thank God, you're alive!" I'm so relieved. He leans closer and totally unexpectedly plants a kiss on my mouth.

"Hey, what are you doing?" I stammer. Without answering my question he takes my face in his hands and fixes me with a piercing look in his eyes. Sighing with relief he pulls me close. Green mountains and rivers pass us by. Are we traveling? In a flash I see myself with a little boy and a little girl. The sudden feeling of bliss is shattered when I fall into a dark tunnel.

"Darn," I cry out, realizing this soul hunt will probably not only be all a bed of roses; it's time for the dark regions of my soul to manifest themselves. With a loud splash I fall into a liquid mass and slowly sink to the bottom. So that was it then. When I gulp up for air I end up swallowing some of it and realize the syrupy stuff has a bittersweet taste. Haha! I know exactly what that is! It's cacao. I've ended up in a pool of melted chocolate! I swim to the surface and see a thin strip of sunlight high above me.

"Enjoy, Lied," I hear the voices of my father and my deceased grandma echo through the hollow space.

Shola is slowly beating her shaman drum. The journey is apparently not over yet. Good, because there's still one question I'm seeking an answer to: Will I one day write a book? Foot-high wall units pop up with thousands of books all neatly stacked next to each other. "Naupaka," says the cover. And then I'm back on the cliffs with a view of the immense ocean. Large sea eagles fly over me on their way to the other side of the world. When I take a closer look I notice they're not birds but books, with the jackets flapping like wings in the air.

Shola gently touches my hand. "Feel free to stay lying down for a while," she whispers. "Whenever you're ready to get up, no rush."

It doesn't take long before I decide to push the blindfold

away, carefully massaging my eyes with my finger tips and get into the lotus position. I regard the slender Italian woman with a huge smile on my face and burst out laughing. She looks at me baffled, and then starts to giggle as well, although still a little uncomfortably.

"It's the first time someone comes out of a soul hunt like that," she chuckles. "Most people are either quiet or sad."

I tell Shola about my experiences; about all the connections I saw between what happened and my stay here on Big Island, and about the visions. She doesn't say anything for a while, letting it sink in. "Over this coming period you will relive certain situations. Old acquaintances will probably show up again. It's all part of the healing process of the lost part of your soul that has to find its way back." She tells me about an ancient Hawaiian ritual of forgiveness, Ho'oponopono, which I can use to feel through fixed patterns and emotions in order to then let go of them permanently and move on.

"Focus on the relevant area or emotion and then repeat the following sentences three times: *I am sorry, please forgive me, I love you, thank you.*"

I repeat those words and throw my arms around her to thank her. Will I see Shola again when I return to Big Island? And what about the long man from my soul hunt, the protector of this area, the one Ku also knows, as he told me after my healing? For me this once again reaffirms that our world is not the only existing one, that there's another world out there with dimensions that go far beyond our stars. If only I could one day take a look there. But first there's another trip waiting for me: my return flight to The Netherlands.

PART 4
BECOMING WHOLE
THE NETHERLANDS
FALL 2013
FLOWER FULLFILLMENT

33 Shine!

As soon as I enter the living room I smell the sweet aroma of warm dough, apples and cinnamon. "Oh, that smells delicious!" I tell my mother, who's just opened the oven to take out an apple pie.

"Yummy, right? This will make a nice treat for when we come back from the forest tomorrow."

I've been looking forward to this day for the past three months. We're going to plant summer oaks; one for my father and one for Sander. It feels good to commemorate them in the presence of my dearest family members.

"But of course we could always take a small slice for dessert later on." My mother winks while she's about to serve a delicious dish of cod fish with lemon juice, parsley and olive oil. An hour later we're both sitting on the couch digesting the copious meal when I start to feel anxious. I walk in and out of the living room several times and end up retreating to my bedroom with a book. As I'm unable to focus on the words I decide to meditate. I close my eyes and straighten up in the lotus position. Almost immediately the image of a bottle of vodka pops up. *That can only be Sander.*

"Hi, Lide," I hear him say.

"Is that you, San?"

"Well, you can see me, can't you?" I look into his playful blue-grey eyes and caress the bristles on his cheek with my hand. I could look at this face for hours... God, he's handsome.

He pulls me close and holds me like that for a good long while. "Do you want a sip of this heavenly concoction?" He points at the bottle in his hand. "You'll love it." When he hands me the bottle I notice it's filled with tiny sparkles of light that are whizzing all over the place. "Stardust" is how Sander describes the contents.

"Okay, I'll take a small sip." I take a little bit of the liquid in my mouth. The room immediately starts to spin like a whirlwind, changing into a kaleidoscope of colored squares and triangles that multiply and take on different shapes in the mirrors. And then we suddenly find ourselves on a terrace with a view of a fir forest and snow-topped mountains. I recognize this place: this is Austria, where we used to go skiing! The valley below us is filled with fluffy clouds that are lit up by the sun. Sander looks at me and gives me a long kiss. His lips feel familiar and good. Out of breath, I have to move my face away from his. I'm confused. This is what I've been longing for. So why am I feeling like this?

"Li, you will first have to feel love within yourself again before you can share it." He takes my hand and in a flash we're back in our little house in Utrecht, The Netherlands. I'm crying in his arms. "Why don't you come and lie down on the couch with me?" he asks. As soon as we cuddle up together I feel my body relax. We've lain like this so often, and not just when Sander was ill, but also when we were waiting for the results of some kind of medical exam. In this position we were able to lower our heart-rate and adrenaline levels. Sander is softly drumming on my head with his fingertips, just like he used to do when we first met. He would always be tapping something or other: the table, the chairs, as well as my head. He was forever looking for a rhythm or a beat, somewhere, anywhere.

"I'm a superb drummer now, you know." He has read my thoughts and kisses my hair.

The next morning the whole house smells of freshly baked croissants. This is so typical of my mother. On the table there's a big plate of warm rolls, a cooked egg, fresh orange juice and Lapsang Souchong tea. I momentarily recall J.'s healthy chocolate smoothies on Big Island. Everything in front of me now would fall into the category of "devilish food" but I decide to gobble up one those sinful croissants all the same. My mother is hunched behind her laptop. The white glare of the screen lights up her sleep-wrinkled face and tousled hair. "Good morning, sweetheart," she greets me. "The weather report predicts showers and gusty wind. It'll be a pretty slushy affair today."

"Oh no it isn't! We're going to get a lot of sunshine and a light breeze," I react joyfully, just like my Hawaiian teachers have taught me.

A few hours later we are walking on the Ramenberg-hill in Eerbeek, Gelderland; the province where I was born and raised. And we're not the only ones. But despite the crowds Tree Day feels remarkably relaxed. This commemoration day is an initiative of the Dutch conservation agency Natuurmomenten, to give people the opportunity to plant trees in remembrance of loved ones, to celebrate births or to plant a so-called "tree of connection". A blond guy with tight fitting jeans, a trench coat and Ray Ban sunglasses walks by lugging a small tree behind him. I notice the sign that is attached to the trunk with a ribbon with two names and a little heart on it - clearly a "love tree". They've lit large fires near the edge of the forest where people can warm their hands. I see children with bread rolls attached to long willow branches; they remind me of miniature fishing men, dangling their catch into the flames.

We walk on to a tent where we find a large basket filled with tags to attach to the trees. With a green marker I try to make an accurate drawing of a naupaka flower and on the back I draw a red heart with our names: "San & Li 2013". And then I suddenly remember Sander's concoction and quickly add the word "stardust" in the margin. When I hold it at arm's length to examine it I feel a wave of sorrow come over me.

"Hi, Liedje, are you okay?" I hear the cheerful voice of my eldest brother's wife. I quickly dry my tears and get up.

"Hi there, Mariël, yeah, I'm okay." I hug her. "It's just... to see the words like that it's suddenly so real."

Behind her I see my eldest brother Diederick. "Hey, *schwester, wie geht's?*" He teases me by asking me in German how I'm doing.

"*Alles klar!*" I give him a playful nudge in his side to show him I'm fine. "And you? All ready for some digging?"

"Well duh, you mean am I ready to see you women wield the shovel?!"

As soon as my other brother, Marnix, his girlfriend, Irene, and their little boy Daan have joined us we walk up the hill together. The ranger who is waiting for us leads us to an already dug hole in the ground where we first plant Sander's summer oak tree. When my three-year old nephew carefully stomps on the soil around the wispy little trunk, I can't hold back the tears any longer. Which is strange because I don't really feel sad. Mariël softly squeezes my hand and throws me a loving, understanding look. When she sees the sign on the tree she turns to me, surprised: "Stardust?! That's the title of a song by De Jeugd van Tegenwoordig, a group we just listened to in the car!" Irene enthusiastically joins in: "And we sung it last night!" I'm flabbergasted. Sander has showered us all with his stardust.

Mariël has meanwhile found the lyrics on her mobile and recites:

"Even though one day I will be "deadde"
You will know I'm somewhere
'Cause I will be there all the same
floating in the air like stardust. "

We look at each other incredulously.

When later that evening we're pigging out on big plates of take-out Thai, my nephew Daan suddenly cries out "shine" and even repeats the word twice. No one speaks.

"Did he really just say 'shine'?" Mariël asks with eyes as big satellite dishes. That was the last thing Sander told her and Irene when they said goodbye.

"What did you just say, sweetie?" I ask. "I don't know, aunt Li," he answers but whispers the word once again.

Later that evening Marnix hands me a book he takes from his bag. "I thought you might like to read this. It's about a woman who had a near-death experience."

I look at the title: *Dying to be Me: My Journey from Cancer, to Near Death, to True Healing.* I hesitate, turned off by the title. Not another one of those cancer books Sander would have said. When I read the back cover I discover the author, Anita Moorjani, had Hodgkin's Lymphoma, just like Sander. *Hmm, maybe I should give it a try.*

"Thank you," I say, and give my brother a wink. "I have a feeling I was meant to read this."

When I switch off the light a couple of hours later, I suddenly remember the book again. I'm instantly wide awake. I turn the light back on and open it. I leaf through the first hundred pages or so, which are about the disease, but chapter 8 in which the author writes about her near-death experience in detail, catches my interest.

"Imagine a huge, dark warehouse. That's where you live and you only have one flashlight to light your way. Everything you know about what's contained in this vast space is what you've seen by the beam of that one tiny flashlight. Now imagine that one day someone suddenly turns the light on. Then, for the first time ever, you see the entire warehouse in an explosion of flashing lights and sound and color. It's totally different from what you had imagined it to look like. Music floods the room with fantastic, kaleidoscopic, spacious-sounding melodies you've never heard before."

Wait a minute, the light switch! I can hardly breathe. "It's like turning flicking a light switch, that's how swiftly it goes," is what Sander told me via Aunty. I heave a deep sigh and remember what Pele whispered to me on the edge of the volcano: "Hulu", the boundary between the physical and the spiritual world is an illusion.

34   Stardust

I just can't shake Sander's
stardust off anymore. It stays in
my mind, especially now that everywhere on the streets and in the houses
in the Utrecht borough of Zuilen where I
live, small starry lights have popped up everywhere. In a few days everywhere around the
world people will cuddle up under a Christmas tree
with their loved ones and families. This year there
are two men missing in my life: Sander and my father.

I take a bite of my homemade muffin while staring across the street at the neighbor's living room. The
lights in their Christmas tree are blinking somewhat
chaotically. I've been working like a monk on my book
for months now but without feeling lonely. "Naupaka,
San." He reacts by tapping.

Outside I hear a little bell. I look out the window and
see two singing garbage men decked out as Santa Claus
throwing garbage bags into their truck. The bell reminds
me of the enormous protector in Big Island, who came
into Shola's little house during my soul hunt. He's the
gateway to the other dimension, to the cosmic world.

"You will learn more about the healing rituals of
the island." I recall Ku's words as well as Aunty
Mahealani's, the Hawaiian medicine woman,
who also said I would one day return to the
island and tell the world about the path
I've chosen and about the lessons I'm
learning.

I open the Word file

"Naupaka" on my laptop.
What lessons have I learned? My
thoughts go back to Hawaii.

The most beautiful lesson was something Ku told me: "Let go of all things that
no longer serve you. Do this with full confidence, because there's always something more
beautiful waiting on the horizon."

However, the trick is to really let go of those
things you want to get rid of. The ancient Ho'oponopono ritual of forgiveness is one of the ways to help
you achieve this: "I am sorry, please forgive me, I love
you, thank you."

Outside a little brown-black cat jumps up on the window sill. She's staring at me; it's Miss Alley Cat, Sander's
favorite street cat. I tap on the window with my fingernail.
"Hi there, girlie. Your big friend no longer lives here. He
changed address." The kitty cat regards me a moment
longer, jumps back onto the sidewalk and moves on. The
cat symbolizes self-love, I suddenly recall.

And then suddenly it all falls into place. With Sander's
death a part of me has died. His death tore my heart
in two, just like the naupaka flower. On Big Island
I rediscovered self-love and self-confidence.

For me writing this book was a healing journey. By writing down the lessons I healed
my own heart, like the naupaka flower.
And that proves the legend is still
very much alive and kicking.

FOR DAD AND SAN

What remains will be the love
that moves the heavens,
the stars,
people,
flowers,
insects,
the love that obliges us all
to walk across dangerous ice
the love that fills us
with joy and with fear,
but gives meaning to everything.

Paulo Coelho, De Zahir

MAHALO NUI LOA

(Thank you very much)

Mom, for taking me under your wing when I came back to The Netherlands.

My brother Diederick, for coaching me in entrepreneurship and for making Naupaka possible.

My brother Marnix, for always picking up when I call.

My dear sisters-in-law Irene and Mariël, and my nephews Daan and Mels, for shining so beautifully together.

A really big aloha-hug to my dear friends, thanking you for all your support and love: Akiko, Annemieke, Aunty Mahealani, Bob, Ester, In-Soo, Ku, Marjolein, Marloes, Maureen, Nienke and Saar. And my soul mate Matthijs, for your sometimes strict but always encouraging words.

My best friend and incredibly talented designer Roel, who dared to go on this adventure with me and never faltered in his belief in Naupaka.

Floor, who brought the flower on the cover of this book to life, and to Lonneke, who made it into a beautiful piece of jewelry.

A special thank you to my editor and friend Manon who, like a veritable stonemason added structure to the book and worked day and night fine-tuning it to the very last detail. My hotline.

Esmir, who crossed my path in a very extraordinary manner and who gave Naupaka the very last nudge towards publication.

Sanne and Onno, for helping me get started.

Margreet, for the first round of corrections and the cozy coffee breaks.

Annoesjka, for the translation.

Mels, who managed to bring Naupaka to life with his graphical tour de force.

Tamara, the Twitter and Kaua'i-woman, mahalo for your help with the media storm.

And finally, dearest Jorn, Sander's best friend, who made the book launch in the Westerliefde in Amsterdam a fact; the very place where Sander and I wanted to organize our huge wedding party.

You've helped me accomplish my dream.

Lobi.

www.naupaka.nl
facebook.com/naupakaboek